1.2 What are the three rock groups?

CW01664828

This is about igneous rocks.

1 Complete the sentences below. Use the words in the box to help you.

lock	lava	slowly	melt	crystals	magma	hot	quickly

The missing words are:

Deep in the ground it is so hot that minerals in the rock melt giving a liquid called magma. The magma then often rises and cools. It may cool slowly below ground and the minerals form large crystals which lock together forming rocks like granite. Some magma does reach the earth's surface, and spurts out of volcanoes as lava. This then cools quickly to form rocks like basalt.

2 Igneous rock forms when rock melts, then cools and hardens once again. The elements that make up all rocks are never created or destroyed; instead they are constantly being recycled.

In the box below design a logo or symbol that could be used tell people this fact about rocks – the oldest recycling machine on the planet! Be as creative and inventive as you can!

The logo or symbol should help explain to people that rocks are constantly recycled, through changes in temperature, or through weathering and erosion.

1.3 What is weathering?

This is about weathering and how it shapes rocks.

1 Lions are the kings of the jungle because of their raw power and strength; however, nothing can stop the weather!

Look at the picture of the stone lion which is found in the city of Nottingham. Over many years, the lion will slowly wear away because of weathering. Describe how different the lion might look in 500 years. What would the lion think about it?!

The lion's face will become smooth and its features will begin to wear away. You may not be able to make out its eyes, mouth or nose as the heat, rain and wind will all affect it. As it is in the city it may also be affected by chemicals in the air caused by cars and lorries. The lion would not be happy because it will lose its identity. It will no longer be the king of the jungle, just a mass of unrecognisable stone.

Answers should describe how different the lion might look, and also describe how the lion might feel about the changes that have happened. An example is given on the left.

2 Write your own definition of the three main types of weathering. Use your definitions to play charades with somebody else in your class. Can they guess which type of weathering you are acting out?

Physical weathering is caused by the effects of changing pressure, temperature, water or ice, slowly making rock break apart.

Chemical weathering is when minerals in the rock undergo chemical reactions, helping to weaken and break it up.

Biological weathering is the weakening and breaking up of rock by plants, animals and microorganisms.

5th edition

geog.3

workbook

answer book

<justin woolliscroft>
<katy patchwood>

OXFORD
UNIVERSITY PRESS

Great Clarendon Street, Oxford, OX2 6DP, United Kingdom

Oxford University Press is a department of the University of Oxford. It furthers the University's objective of excellence in research, scholarship, and education by publishing worldwide. Oxford is a registered trade mark of Oxford University Press in the UK and in certain other countries

Authors: Justin Woolliscroft, Katy Patchwood

The moral rights of the authors have been asserted

Database right Oxford University Press (maker)

First published 2006

New editions published 2009 and 2015

This edition published 2023

British Library Cataloguing in Publication Data
Data available

ISBN 978-0-19-848994-8

10 9 8 7 6 5 4 3 2 1

Paper used in the production of this book is a natural, recyclable product made from wood grown in sustainable forests.

The manufacturing process conforms to the environmental regulations of the country of origin.

Printed in Great Britain by Ashford Colour Press Ltd, Gosport.

MIX
Paper from responsible sources
FSC www.fsc.org FSC® C011748

Acknowledgements

The publisher and authors would like to thank the following for permission to use photographs and other copyright material:

Photos: p6: Mark Richardson / Alamy Stock Photo; **p10:** Richard Baker / Alamy Stock Photo; **p15:** Logo usage with kind permission from WaterAid; WaterAid is a registered charity: England and Wales 288701, Scotland SC039479; **p29:** Andrew Cole / Alamy Stock Photo; **p33:** Our World in Data (CC BY 4.0); **p46(a):** PORNCHAI KITTIWONGSAKUL/AFP/ Getty Images; **p46(b):** ROMEO GACAD/AFP via Getty Images; **p46(c):** A.S. Zain / Shutterstock; **p46(d):** Bullit Marquez / Associated Press / Alamy Stock Photo; **p48:** Antonio Capone/AGF/Universal Images Group/Getty Images; **p50:** Holger Mette / iStock; **p51:** Images & Stories / Alamy Stock Photo.

Artwork by Q2A Media, Phoenix Photosetting, Barking Dog Art, Ian West, Mike Phillips, Szilvia Szakall, Simon Tegg Illustration, Mike Connor, and Oxford University Press.

Some pages or activities in this edition are based on material written by Anna King, Catherine Hurst, and Katherine James for the original edition.

Note that the content of any direct speech attributed to characters in this book is based on information from reliable sources.

Contents

From rock to soil

1.1 Our rocky home

This is about the rocks that are beneath our feet.

1 Complete the crossword to show your knowledge of rocks. Use the information on pages 6–7 in the student book to help you.

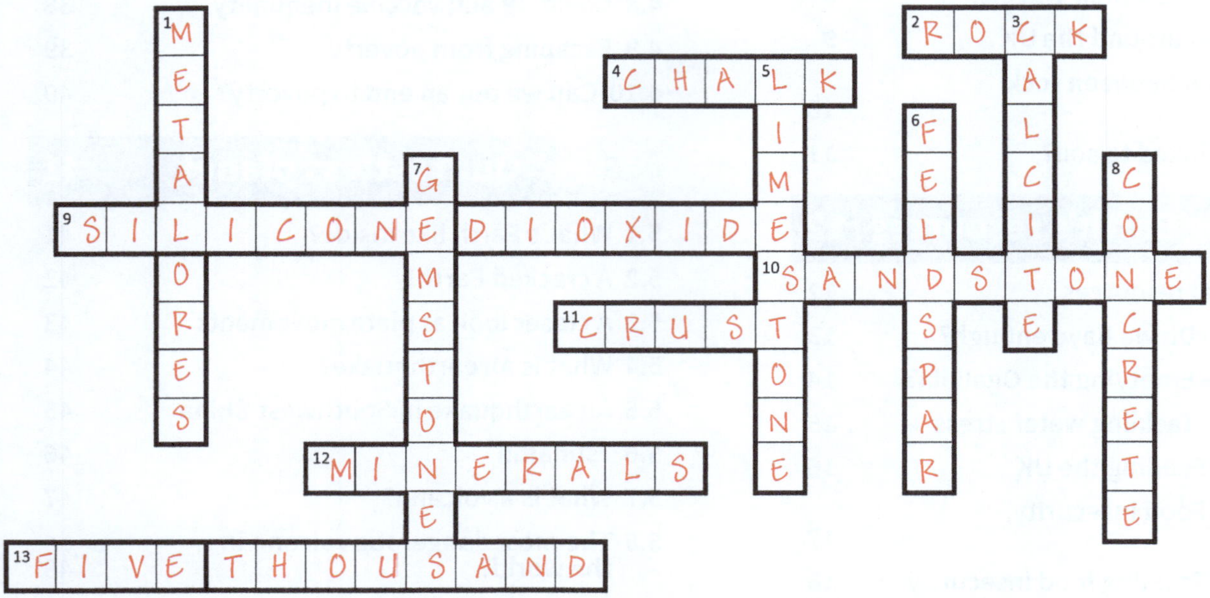

Clues

Across

2 A mixture of minerals

4 A common form of limestone

9 Another name for quartz

10 This rock is mainly quartz. The crystals are very small

11 The hard outer layer of the Earth

12 Natural compound that forms rocks

13 The number of known minerals

Down

1 Rocks from which we get metals

3 Another name for calcium carbonate

5 Rock that is mainly calcium carbonate

6 Minerals made of silicon and oxygen

7 Attractive minerals such as diamond, ruby or jade

8 Material made of crushed rock and sand

2 Go to the British Geological Survey's website and look up the Geology Viewer tool. Find out what rocks lie beneath your feet and write a description of the geology of your area below.

An example could be:

I live near York. This is a sandstone area but on top of the rock there is clay, together with quite a lot of sand and gravel.

1.4 What is the rock cycle?

Here you will learn more about why 'recycling rocks'!

1 Draw a line to match each word with its meaning.

Word	***Meaning***
Magma	liquid rock at or above the Earth's surface
Erosion	particles of eroded rock or plant and animal debris
Sediment	liquid rock below the Earth's surface
Lava	the process of wearing away rocks

2 Are these statements true or false? Put a tick in the correct box.

		True	**False**
a	The hard outer part of Earth is cracked into huge slabs, called plates	✓	
b	Some slabs collide because of plate movements	✓	
c	The rock cycle destroys materials such as granite		✓
d	Diamonds form when magma cools in sedimentary rock		✓
e	Weathering leads to soil	✓	

3 Describe in your own words what the diagram below shows.

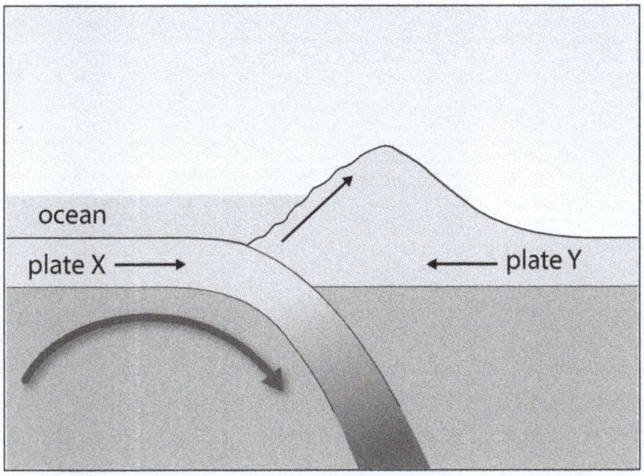

As plate X and plate Y move together and collide, plate X is forced downwards.
As it goes down into the earth the rock turns into metamorphic rock and
eventually melts. The collision makes plate Y rise up into mountains.

1.5 The British Isles on their travels!

Here you will explore the geological timescale.

1 Printed below are nine events that have happened in geological history. Put them in the correct order by writing a number from 1–9 at the start of each box.

7 Dinosaurs become extinct	8 Mammals and birds thrive	2 First animals with shells appear
1 First living cells appear in sea	3 Giant insects emerge	6 First birds appear
4 Warm-blooded reptiles appear	5 Dinosaurs first appear	9 Humans appear and spread

2 Using the words in the boxes and information from page 15 in **geog.3** to help you, write a paragraph describing how the earth evolved. Remember to use years and the correct names of the geological periods in your answer.

In pre-Cambrian times the first living cells appeared in the sea. This was 3.5 billion years ago! Around 540 million years ago the first animals with shells appeared in the sea, and giant, scary insects appeared in the Carboniferous period. The first warm-blooded reptiles appeared around 290 million years ago and then the first dinosaurs appeared in the Triassic period. The first birds arrived 200 million years ago and then at the end of the Cretaceous period, the dinosaurs died out and became extinct. After this mammals and birds grew in numbers. Humans only appeared on Earth about 2.6 million years ago, so we were really very, very late!

Rock and relief around the UK

Here you will find out some more about the mountains in the UK.

1 Read the following descriptions of mountains in the UK. Use an atlas and do your research to find out the name of each of the mountains, and their relative height (their height in relation to their surrounding). Write your answers in the table below.

Who am I?	Mountain name	Relative height in metres
I am on the west coast of Scotland at the western end of the Grampian mountains. I am close to the town of Fort William, and am proud to be the tallest mountain in the British Isles.	Ben Nevis	1344 metres
I am the highest mountain in northern Scotland, north of the Great Glen. I am found west-south-west of Inverness. I am very isolated, lying 10km from the nearest road.	Carn Eige	1147 metres
I can be found near the town of Porthmadoc in north Wales. There is a national park named after me. I am the highest point in the British Isles outside of Scotland. I have a railway too!	Snowdon	1038 metres
I am found right in the middle of the Cairngorms National Park and am the second highest mountain in the United Kingdom. They say that I am haunted by a big Grey Man, but I'm not telling!	Ben Macdui	950 metres
Hello! You will find me in the English county of Cumbria and I am the highest mountain in England! Climb me on a clear day, and you can see Scotland, Wales, Ireland, and the Isle of Man! I am found to the east of Wastwater, one of the famous lakes in the Lake District National Park.	Scafell Pike	912 metres
I am found between Thirlmere and Ullswater, two lakes in the Lake District National Park. I lie north-east of the highest mountain in England and south-east of Keswick.	Helvellyn	712 metres

2 On the map below the six mountains are numbered 1–6. Write the name of each mountain in the space next to the number.

Number	Mountain name
1	Snowdon
2	Scafell Pike
3	Carn Eige
4	Helvellyn
5	Ben Nevis
6	Ben Macdui

1.7 What's the link between rock and landscape?

Here you will find out some more about limestone landscapes.

1 How does the acid found in rain affect the limestone?

Rainwater is naturally a little acidic because ***carbon dioxide*** from the air dissolves in it. The acid in the rain has a chemical reaction with the limestone, which is mainly made up of calcium carbonate. As the rain soaks down into cracks in the rock it dissolves as it goes.

2 Why is the soil thin in limestone areas?

The soil is thin in limestone areas because, as the rock weathers, it dissolves. This leaves little material to help form soil.

Grykes are gaps in a limestone pavement formed as the limestone dissolves

Clints are blocks of limestone that are left when the limestone around them dissolves

Tip!

As the limestone dissolves, it often leaves gaps where the joints in the limestone are. It can form a limestone pavement as shown in the photograph. The gaps are called *grykes* and the blocks are called *clints*.

3 Annotate the photograph above to show where the grykes and clints are found. For each, explain how they are formed.

4 Many limestone areas have underground caves. Why do you think caves form underground?

As the rain falls, it dissolves the minerals in the limestone. Limestone contains many cracks. As the groundwater moves deep underground through these cracks, they become larger. Over a long period of time, a cavern may form, which may be connected to many smaller caves.

1.8 How are *you* linked to soil?

Here you will find out why worms are so important.

Hello, I'm Willow the worm!

I have such a busy life, even though I move quite slowly. I have even been called an 'ecosystem engineer'! I can make burrows that are vertical or go sideways, allowing all that lovely oxygen and water to come into the soil.

I don't have a problem choosing what to eat, like you humans do – if it is rotting, decaying, or organic I will want to have a taste! A lot of my day is spent 'decomposing' – eating and breaking up organic matter such as dead plants and animals so that bacteria and fungi can feed on it and release the lovely nutrients back into the soil. With all this eating it is not surprising that I leave behind castings that are a very valuable type of fertiliser. And that's not all, because as I move I also mix up the soil layers. A famous scientist called Charles Darwin called us 'nature's ploughs' and others have called us 'tiny food processors'!

1 Why do you think worms have been called 'ecosystem engineers'?

Worms constantly burrow, mix, and fertilise, so they are vital to the formation of soil, and therefore vital to plants and humans. Without their work the ecosystem would not function.

2 How can worm burrows help plants grow?

Burrows loosen up the soil so roots can grow into the ground more easily.

3 Where do the nutrients come from that go back into the soil after the worm spends its time decomposing?

Every organism eats food that contains nutrients. As these organisms die, the nutrients that are left in them are passed back into the soil.

4 Why do you think Darwin called worms 'nature's ploughs'? Do you think that's a good name for them? Why?

The correct answer is on the right, but if students do not think that's a good name for them, they should be given credit for a plausible answer.

Worms naturally mix the soil and organic matter, help it absorb and hold water, and increase its fertility. This is very similar to the plough that a farmer uses to break up the soil to bring fresh nutrients to the surface.

5 In the space below draw a poster that tells people why worms are so important. Be as creative as you can!

Responses to Q5 should include information in Unit 1.8 of **geog.3** and this page in the workbook.

Using Earth's resources

2.1 Earth's natural resources

Here we look at our basic needs and the resources used to cover them.

This Earth we live on provides us with our basic needs (see page 24 in **geog.3**):

Water Food Clothing Shelter Energy

1 Write down how your own basic needs are met.

Water

Food

Clothing

Shelter

Energy

Most students will describe a situation where their needs are met by a mixture of government provision (social housing), utility companies (water and energy), and by access to the market (clothing, food, and private housing).

2 Can you define the following terms and give an example of each?

a Natural resource: something which occurs naturally and which we can make use of.

Example: soil, water, wind, sunlight, coal, oil...

b Renewable resource: resource that we can keep using and will not run out.

Example: sunlight, wind...

c Non-renewable resource: resource of which there is only a finite amount in Earth.

Example: copper, oil, coal...

3 The world's population keeps rising. Why does this pose a challenge when it comes to resources?

When the world's population rises, there is a higher demand for water, food and energy. Not everyone has access to what they need, as resources are limited and not evenly distributed.

Water part 1 – Do we have enough?

This is about how increasing population and wealth affect water use.

1 Over the next 30 years, the global demand for water is expected to increase.

Water use	2030 (% change)	2050 (% change)
Farming	−3.6	−6.9
Industry	+53.3	+119.8
Domestic Use	+36.5	+65.1

Add the three missing bars to the graph, using data from the table.

Completed graph looks like:

Predicted Global Trends in Water Use 2030–2050

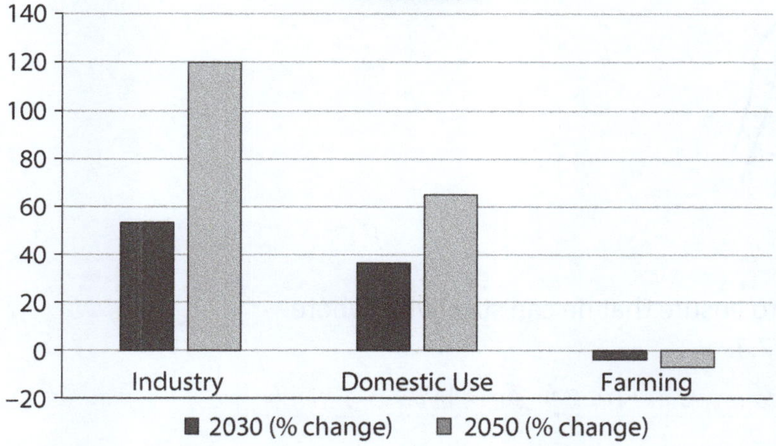

2 Earth's population is increasing rapidly. Explain how this may affect:

Industrial water use *To support a larger population, there will be an increase in the production of materials used for buildings, roads and utilities. Food processing and packaging will increase.*

→ More consumer goods will be made. This increase in industry will translate into an increase in water use.

Domestic water use *More people means more water will be used in homes; for drinking, washing, cooking, cleaning, etc.*

3 People are becoming richer, and the middle class is expanding. Explain how this may affect:

Industrial water use *As wages rise, people can afford more consumer goods. More people will be able to afford holidays, so there may be an increase in the aviation and tourism industries.*

→ This will translate into an increase in water use.

Domestic water use *When people have more money, they can afford to use more water. More homes will have indoor plumbing. More people will have gardens, which they may irrigate.*

4 The data predicts that water use for farming will decrease. What could be the reason for this?

Even though increasing population means increasing demand for food, it is likely that agriculture will become more efficient, thus wasting less water. Crops grown using GMO techniques can be engineered to require less water.

Water part 2 – Emptying the Ogallala?

Here we look at the future for farmers when their underground irrigation water runs out.

1 What ideas do you think Brad might come up with to ensure that he can stay living where he is? Check your ideas against suggestions in unit 2.4.

Examples of how to utilise scarce water resources are given in unit 2.4. Brad lives in a highly developed country, so using technology to introduce sophisticated irrigation systems is one possibility for him – as is growing crops that need less water.

2 Find out where the largest groundwater aquifer in the world is. What makes it less likely to run out of water in the near future compared to the Ogallala?

The largest aquifer in the world is the Great Artesian Basin in Australia. The population of Australia is far less than that of the USA so there is less demand for its water.

Water part 3 – Tackling water stress

Here we look at how the problem of economic water scarcity is being addressed.

WaterAid

WaterAid is an international organisation whose mission is to transform the lives of the poorest and most marginalised people by improving access to safe water, sanitation, and hygiene.

1 Find out about WaterAid. Write down in your own words what its aims are.

Answers will vary. Students could mention the use of water in bathrooms and kitchens. They could suggest shorter showers, reusing rain water to water indoor plants, checking taps for leaks, etc.

2 Make a list of the different ways in which WaterAid has set about achieving its mission.

Students can go to the WaterAid website for this information. Their activities fall into three broad divisions; delivering services, making change happen and generating support.

3 Think about your day to day life. How much water do you use in a day? What could you change to reduce your water consumption?

Answers will vary. Students could mention the use of water in bathrooms and kitchens. They could suggest shorter showers, reusing rain water to water indoor plants, checking taps for leaks, etc.

4 Define the following terms:

a harvesting pond pond that collects runoff rainwater, for example from rooftops, and stores it.

b drip irrigation system to water crops in which the water runs beside or under the plants, in flexible tubes, and drips out through tiny holes.

c desalination process used to turn salty sea water into fresh water.

2.5 Food part 1 – Feeding the UK

Here we look at food security in the UK.

1 Overall, around 64% of the food we eat in the UK is produced here, while the rest is imported. Look at the list of food items below, and decide whether the UK mostly produces them or imports them. Then, draw each food item in the correct box.

wheat	banana	egg	tea	orange	lemon	potato

Food largely produced in the UK	Food largely imported by the UK
Students should have drawn: wheat egg potato	Students should have drawn: banana tea orange lemon

2 Write one advantage and one disadvantage of food imports. Answers will vary.

Advantage: a wider range of food

Disadvantage: tariffs on trades with countries outside the EU, potential trade wars, bigger impact on the environment

3 What impact could climate change have on food security in the UK? List at least two possible consequences.

Climate change brings extreme weather, such as heatwaves and floods, which presents a problem for British farmers. The rise of temperatures in the UK also means that crops, and farm animals could be affected by new pests and diseases.

4 One of the changes the UK could make to become more self-sufficient in food is use hydroponics. Explain what that consists of.

Plants are grown in water containing the nutrients they need. No soil is used, and LED lights can provide artificial sunlight.

Food part 2 – Food insecurity, a global issue

This is about food insecurity, and the issues that lead to it.

1 Decide whether these statements are true or false, then put a tick in the correct box.

	True	False
a Some countries with high levels of food insecurity have lots of farmers.	✓	
b Famine and food insecurity are the same thing.		✓
c The only factors linked to food insecurity are poverty levels.		✓
d Poor infrastructure can make it harder to distribute food.	✓	

2 If you marked any of the statements from exercise 1 as false, explain why they are incorrect.

b. Famine is the most extreme case of food insecurity. It is possible for a group of people to experience food insecurity and not famine. c. Pests and diseases, conflict, climate change and water stress can all be linked to food insecurity.

3 Look at this world map, which shows hunger (a strong indicator of food insecurity) around the world.

Hunger around the world

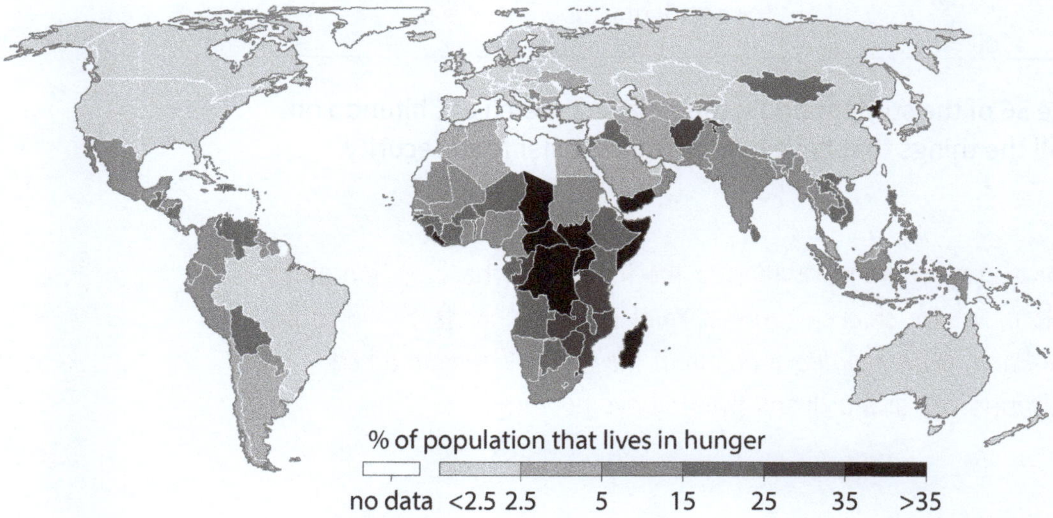

As you can see, hunger is not distributed evenly around the world. In the countries coloured in a darker shade, many people suffer from food insecurity. Why do you think that is? List at least three factors that contribute to food insecurity there.

Possible answers are: Poverty is a big issue in those countries, so people can't afford to buy enough food, and farmers can't afford what they need to get good crops. Poor roads and no electricity make it hard to move food and store it safely. There is conflict in the area, which can affect the production and movement of food. It's a very dry area, so water stress is a problem there. Climate change has made droughts more frequent.

2.7 Food part 3 – Tackling food insecurity

This is about ways to achieve food security in developing countries.

1 Food security is when people have access, at all times, to the food they need.

In each of the boxes below, write a sentence explaining how people in developing countries can get more food security by using farming methods, technology, and storing food.

Use at least two of these words and phrases in each sentence. Tick them off when you have used them:

☐ sacks	☐ artificial intelligence	☐ drones	☐ insects
☐ fertiliser	☐ satellites	☐ seeds	☐ rainwater pits

Farming methods

NGOs offer training for farmers and may also provide them with loans of **fertiliser** and drought resistant **seeds**. Planting in **pits** helps to trap and store rainwater.

Food storage

Food can be stored in **sacks** which have been designed to keep out **insects** and mould, so that it stays fresh.

Technology

Artificial intelligence can study images of farms, taken by **satellites** or **drones**. It can spot diseases which may be spreading, and compare soil moisture levels. During the pandemic, this technology was used to help those most in need, by identifying the poorest quality housing, and sending food vouchers to the residents' mobile phones.

2 Read about Chifundo on page 36 of the student book, then make a sketch of Chifundo on her farm in Malawi. Include all the things that have helped improve her food security. Label each feature.

Student's sketches should be a creative interpretation of the things they have written about in the boxes above. Chifundo may have chickens and sacks of maize at her feet. She could be sprinkling seeds with one hand, while holding a phone in the other. There could be rainwater pits in the fields around her and a drone flying above her head.

2.8 Energy part 1 – Goodbye to the fossil fuels?

This looks at how future generations will judge our reliance on oil.

1 As our use of oil goes up, there are fewer supplies of it left in the ground. Can you think of two reasons for leaving it in the ground for future generations?

We may find better uses for oil in the future than simply burning it to power vehicles. And leaving it in the ground helps to slow down climate change.

2 How do you think students of your age in a hundred years' time will look back on our use of oil?

By 2115 it is likely that all our energy will come from renewable sources (and perhaps nuclear fusion). Students then will look back on the fossil fuel age as wasteful and destructive.

3 You are a writer in the year 2115. By then all our energy will come from renewable sources. Write an article below titled 'The fossil fuel age'.

Students may enjoy this exercise of thinking ahead. Few are likely to paint our age as one of sensible use of resources to generate power, although some may point out that we had little alternative given the size of the population. It is true that currently we are unable to do without fossil fuels, at least in the short term.

Energy part 2 – Renewables in the UK

This is about the natural sources of energy in the UK.

Examples of possible sites for exploiting natural sources of energy are shown on the drawing below.

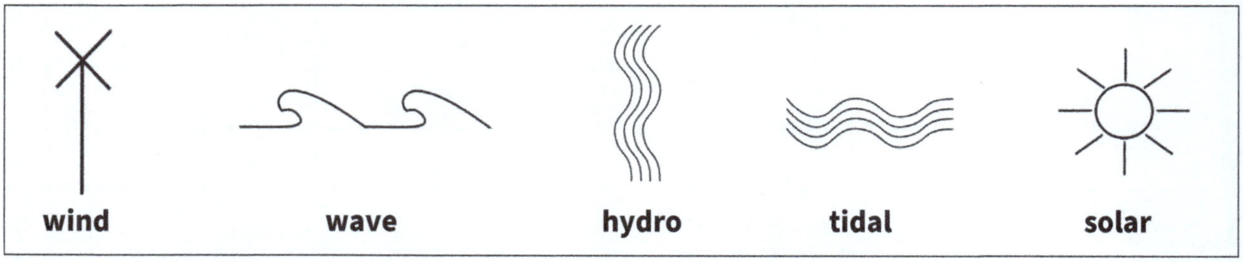

1 Imagine it is 2050. How would this town get its energy? Draw symbols on the town showing what you think should happen.

2 The town has decided to get all of its energy from renewable sources. What problems might there be?

The problems will vary according to the power source. Wind and solar technologies are available but they are intermittent (and solar in the UK is inefficient at certain times of the year). Wave and tidal technologies are in the early stages of development and would involve a large capital outlay. Hydro technology is available but only in certain places. A dam upstream may be possible but would also cost a lot of money to build.

Energy part 3 – Is solar power the solution?

This explains what solar power is, and where it can best be used.

1 Circle the correct word below to complete the sentence.

Solar power means using energy from the SEA / RAIN / SUN / WIND. (SUN circled)

2 Use the map to give the places in the table a ranking for solar power. Give number 1 to the place best suited for solar power, down to 6 for the place least suited.

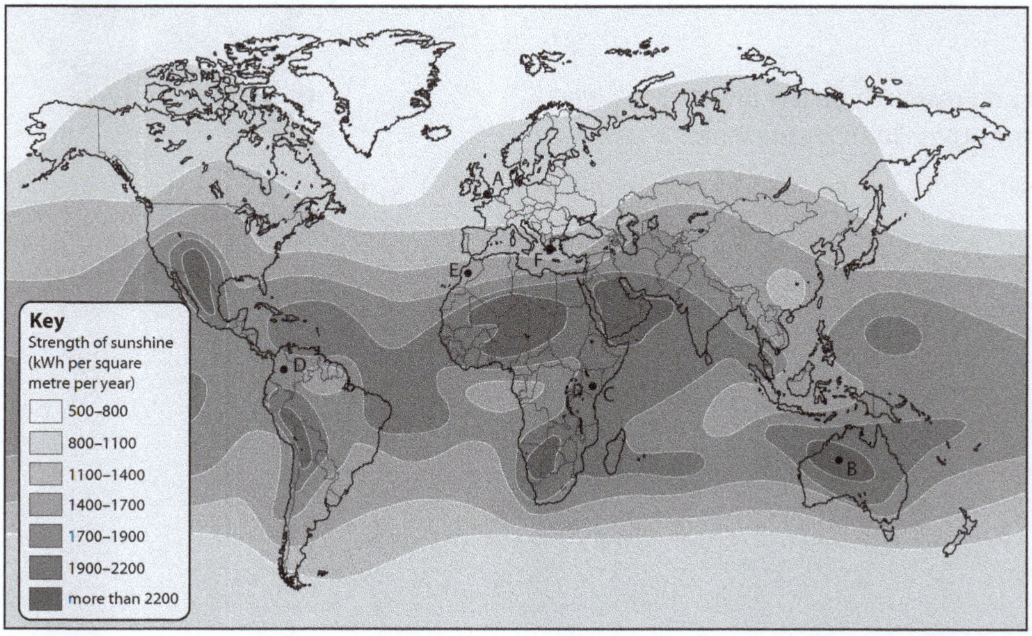

Location on map	Name	Ranking
A	Britain	6
B	Australia	1
C	Kenya	2
D	Colombia	3
E	Morocco	4
F	Greece	5

The rankings should be:
1. Australia
2. Kenya
3. Colombia
4. Morocco
5. Greece
6. Britain

Solar power is useful because the PV cells can convert sunlight into electrical energy on a stand-alone system. This means they don't need to be connected to a national grid and can be sited anywhere (providing there is enough sunlight!).

3 Complete the two speech bubbles for Jomo, a Kenyan schoolboy living in an isolated small village. What does he think about the possibilities of solar power?

My country is sunny all year round, so …

....

....

....

....

My school is miles from anywhere, but …

....

....

....

....

Jomo will say that solar power would suit his country very well and although he lives miles from anywhere, solar power will provide electricity on the spot and connect him with the rest of the world.

2.11 Why must we change our ways?

Here we consider the threats from human activity to biodiversity.

The word that is used to express the number and variety of animal and plant species is 'biodiversity'. One term that is used to express the greatest threats to biodiversity is **HIPPO**, standing for **H**abitat destruction, **I**nvasive species, **P**ollution, human over-**P**opulation, and **O**ver-harvesting.

1 Refer to pages 44–45 in **geog.3** and research on the internet to give examples of each of the categories that HIPPO represents.

Habitat destruction Students will get the information to answer this question partly from Unit 2.11 and also from the internet.

Invasive species

Pollution

human over-**P**opulation

Over-harvesting

Earning a living

3.1 What kind of work do we do, in the UK?

This is about the kind of work people in the UK do for a living.

1 What is an *employment sector*?

An employment sector is where people work in jobs of a similar nature, for example producing raw materials or providing services.

2 a Circle the correct word to complete each sentence.

In the SECONDARY / (PRIMARY) / QUATERNARY sector, people gather materials from the earth.

In the SECONDARY / (QUATERNARY) / TERTIARY sector, people do hi-tech research.

In the PRIMARY / (TERTIARY) / QUATERNARY sector, people provide a service for others.

In the TERTIARY / (SECONDARY) / PRIMARY sector, people turn materials into things to sell.

b Now give two example of jobs in each sector. Answers will vary. Here are some possible answers:

Primary:

farmers, fishermen, miners, oil workers, forestry workers...

Secondary:

factory workers, house builders, people constructing roads and railways...

Tertiary:

teachers, caregivers, cashiers, bus drivers, salespeople...

Quaternary:

researchers, programmers, journalists, product designers...

3 Imagine that there are big strikes in the forestry industry, in the primary sector. Do you think that would have an impact on the secondary sector? Explain why.

Strikes in the forestry industry would have an impact on the secondary sector. It could mean that there is a shortage of materials such as wood, which people working in the secondary sector need to build things.

3.2 The UK's changing pattern of employment

Here we consider what changes in our employment structure lie ahead.

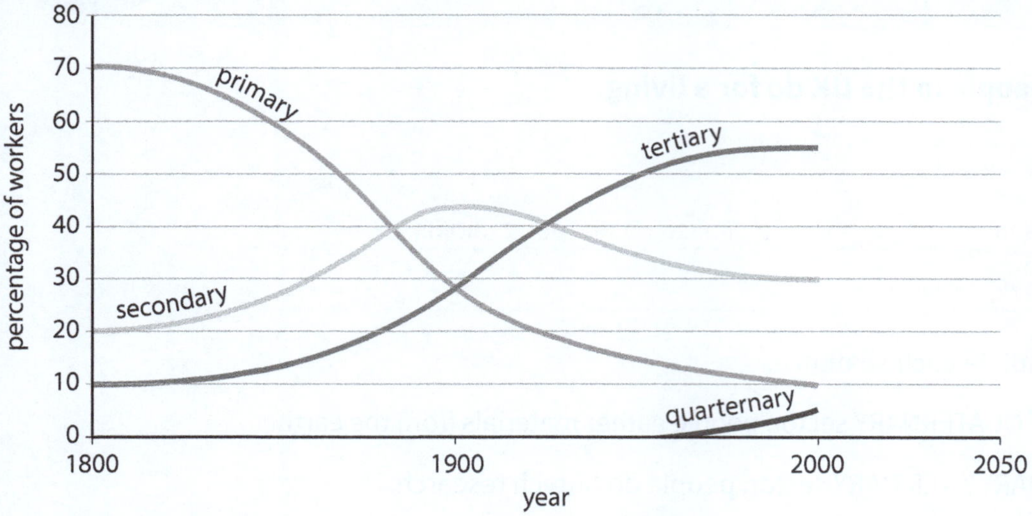

The questions on this page will help inform the students as they consider how to extend the lines on the graph. The important thing for them to realise is that the final position of each sector on the graph must add up to 100%.

Look at the graph, which appeared in **geog.3**. Extend the lines according to how you think the graph might look in 2050. Consider the following:

- Our farmers still produce 60% of the food we eat.
- Manufacturing has started to return to the UK.
- Automation in the service sector is increasing.

Don't forget that the four lines have to add up to 100%!

1 Although our agricultural sector is still an important part of the economy, it represents a very small percentage of the workforce. Why is this?

With the use of machinery and technology, fewer workers are needed in the agricultural sector. Also, the secondary, tertiary, and quaternary sectors kept growing with new jobs being created.

2 Factory workers in less-developed countries are becoming more prosperous. How might this affect manufacturing in the UK?

Manufacturing has already begun to return to the UK for this reason. (Note, changes in the economy and in the world can slow this down).

3 If manufacturing begins to return to the UK, will it provide the same number of jobs as before? If not, why not?

Mechanisation is one way in which manufacturing can compete, but this means a smaller, more highly trained workforce.

4 The UK leads the world in the creation and design of computer games. Why do you think that this activity can be described as part of the quaternary sector?

Gaming is an important hi-tech industry where knowledge and creative skills on the part of everybody involved are necessary. For that reason it can be considered part of the quaternary sector.

3.3 Example: change in and around Doncaster

Here we look at the different sorts of jobs that Doncaster can offer.

Inventive answers should be welcome, but realistic examples are;

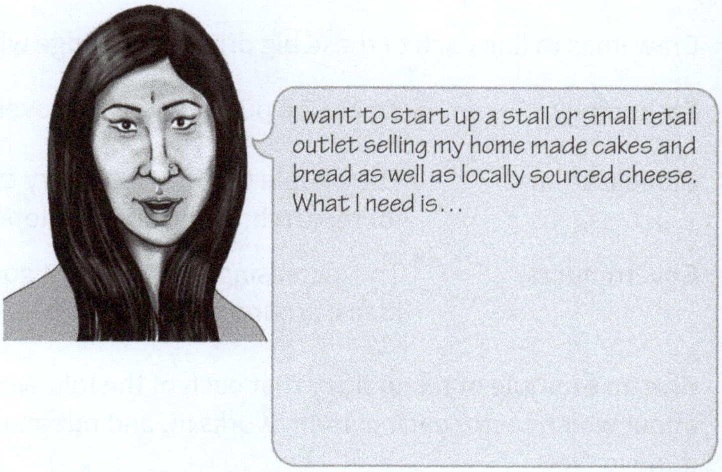

the redundant coalminer will want a job where application and physical work is involved. But he may also be willing to retrain to find the right job. The woman needs money to set up her business, and the software developer wants to work for a hi-tech company.

1 All three of the people above live in Doncaster. Complete their statements.

2 Which of the three is the most likely to leave Doncaster in search of work? Why?

The software developer is most likely to leave in search of work, possibly to London, or one of the big northern cities, where there are more opportunities.

3 Research the tourist attractions in and around Doncaster. Given its long history and the many local attractions, what do you think could be done to boost Doncaster's tourist industry?

Students will need to research the attractions of Doncaster, some of which lie in the city but many of which can be found in the surrounding countryside. So one suggestion could be that companies conducting guided tours with Doncaster as the base could be set up.

3.4 Why do employment patterns change?

This is about the changes in employment patterns and the role that technology played in those.

1 Draw lines to link each of these big drivers of change with its correct definition.

Technology → Where we put scientific discoveries and inventions to practical use.

Globalisation → The increasing movement of goods, services, people money, and ideas, around the world.

Governments → The people that run a country can offer finance for factories, grants for research, grants for development, etc.

2 Give an example of technology that each of the following workers might use. Then, think about which sector each of them works in, and put a tick in the correct box. The first one is done for you.

Answers will vary.

	Primary sector	Secondary sector	Tertiary sector	Quaternary sector
a Scientist: a new powerful microscope				✓
b Builder: e.g. a new bulldozer		✓		
c Farmer: e.g. a big harvester	✓			
d Teacher: e.g. online resources			✓	

3 Look at the boxes you've ticked in the previous exercise. Do you think all sectors have seen some change brought on by technology, or are some of them not affected by it?

Technology has had an impact on all sectors.

4 Do you think that technology has made the percentage of workers in the following sectors go up, down, or has had no effect on it? Draw the correct symbol next to each sector:

The % has gone up: ↑ The % has gone down: ↓ Technology hasn't had an effect: **X**

a Primary sector: ↓

b Secondary sector: ↓

c Tertiary sector: ↑

3.5 A closer look at globalisation and the UK

Here we look at the causes and consequences of globalisation.

1 Read the following comments and decide if each person considers globalisation a benefit or a problem. Then, draw a happy face ☺ or a sad face ☹ accordingly in each circle.

☹ A lovely local business that had been in my town for ages had to close down because it couldn't compete with TNCs. I miss it!

I lost my job in IT because it was cheaper for the company to outsource the work than to pay UK wages. ☹

☺ I work in the hospitality sector and most of my clients are tourists. They bring a lot of money into the country!

We have a wider choice when shopping, and the prices for things made abroad are often lower than for things made in the UK. ☺

2 Containerisation, information technology, and air travel all played a part in globalisation. Pick one, and explain how it played a part.

Answers will vary. Students should mention that containerisation made it easier and cheaper to transport goods, that IT allows people to buy and sell from anywhere and move money in minutes, or that air travel means that many people and cargo move around the world daily.

3 Governments can favour globalisation if it helps their economies, or they can slow it down to protect their industries. Read the following measures and decide it they are in place to push globalisation, or to slow it down.

	Push	**Slow down**
a impose tariffs		✓
b make trade deals	✓	
c refuse work permits to people from overseas		✓
d limit access to social media		✓

4 Can you list some of the ways in which the Covid-19 pandemic slowed down globalisation?

Countries closed their borders, air travel stopped, factories shut down, and world trade in goods fell.

3.6 Is your mobile linked to globalisation?

This is about TNCs and the arguments for and against globalisation.

1 Which employment sectors are involved in transnational corporations (TNCs), such as Apple? Tick all that apply.

The primary sector	✓	The tertiary sector	✓
The secondary sector	✓	The quaternary sector	✓

2 a Look at the table. Decide which arguments are For and which Against globalisation. Circle your answer.

b Then decide which arguments can be described as Social, Economic, or Environmental. You may want to circle more than one possible answer. Answers will vary.

Argument	For or against?	Social (S), economic (Ec), and/or environmental (En)?
Globalisation breaks down barriers between countries.	For / Against	S / Ec / En
Globalsation causes unemployment in some developed countries.	For / Against	S / Ec / En
When a multinational opens a factory in a developing country, it helps that country to develop.	For / Against	S / Ec / En
The activities of some multinationals can pollute an area.	For / Against	S / Ec / En
Multinationals look for the cheapest source of labour.	For / Against	S / Ec / En
Globalisation can change the culture of a developing country.	For / Against	S / Ec / En
The wages earned by people in developing countries help their country to develop.	For / Against	S / Ec / En
Many developing countries do not have adequate laws to make sure the water and air are kept clean.	For / Against	S / Ec / En
Globalisation gives people a wide choice over what they can buy.	For / Against	S / Ec / En
Multinationals help developing countries to exploit their resources.	For / Against	S / Ec / En

3 Select one argument from the table that is for globalisation, and one that is against it. For each one, write a short paragraph to support that argument.

For: Responses will vary. One clear example *for* is 'Globalisation breaks down barriers between countries'.

Against: A clear example *against* is 'multinationals look for the cheapest source of labour'.

3.7 Employment and the shock of Covid-19

This is about changes to working habits during and after the Covid-19 pandemic.

1 During the lockdowns of the Covid-19 outbreak, many adults, students, and children had to do their work at home. Sometimes this was challenging, but there were also some benefits. How was it for you?

Fill in the boxes below. You can write about things such as: family, friends, meals, transport, daily routine, distractions, technology...

Things I found challenging about studying at home...	Benefits of studying at home....
Students can write about many things but could mention things such as: conflict with family, less time with friends, missing the outdoors, lethargy, technical difficulties.	Students can write about many things but could mention things such as: more time with family, saving time on travelling, home cooked food, better concentration.

2 Read what Jed has to say about his lifestyle. Fill the speech bubble.

After the pandemic, my boss said I didn't need to go back to the office, so I decided to pack up my laptop and travel around the world for a few months. I can work anywhere with a good Wi-Fi connection. I'm currently in South America. Next stop, Asia! People say I'm a 'digital nomad'.

The best things about this lifestyle are...

Students could write about the exciting opportunities of being free to travel the world while working and meeting travellers from other countries.

But sometimes, it's hard because...

Students could write about missing home, getting sick, poor wifi connections and the discipline of time management.

3 Due to the rise in remote working, some office space is now vacant. Look at this empty office building. Try to come up with five things that the building could be used for now.

Answers will vary. Students could suggest apartments, co-working space, coffee shop, gym, artisan markets, pop-up restaurants, climbing wall, yoga studio, etc.

So what kind of work will *you* do?

This is about green jobs and climate change.

1 Draw lines to match up this list of green jobs with their job descriptions.

Job		Description	Function
a Air quality engineer	**1**	Solves issues such as hazardous waste disposal, soil quality issues, and habitat protection.	P
b Chief sustainability officer	**2**	Researches improvements for farming techniques and developing new food products.	P L
c Environmental consultant	**3**	Monitors the emissions of pollutants in the air, especially in urban areas.	P R
d Hydrologist	**4**	Develops sustainability programmes for businesses and oversees them.	P L R
e Food scientist	**5**	Designs techniques for removing carbon from the atmosphere, including capture of CO_2 from the air and nature-based methods involving forests and microbes.	R
f Wind turbine technician	**6**	Solves complex problems related to water access and quality.	P
g Carbon removal engineer	**7**	Uses electrical and computer skills to maintain wind turbines.	L

(Answers: a – 3, b – 4, c – 1, d – 6, e – 2, f – 7, g – 5)

2 Green jobs have different functions, such as:

- Protecting the environment (**P**). *E.g. Preserving natural resources such as soil, oceans, rivers, air, forests.*
- Limiting climate change (**L**). *E.g. Making global agreements to restrict the use of fossil fuels.*
- Reducing the impacts of climate change (**R**). *E.g. People may grow different crops as the climate gets warmer, cooler, wetter or drier.*

Try to explain the difference between 'limiting climate change' and 'reducing the impacts of climate change.'

'Limiting climate change' means preventing it from getting worse. 'Reducing the impacts of climate change' is about adapting to the difficulties that it creates, rather than trying to stop it.

3 Look at the jobs from exercise 1. What are their functions? Write the letters **P**, **L**, and **R** in the empty boxes to indicate the job function. You can use more than one letter per job; the first one has been done as an example.

International development

4.1 An unequal world

This is about how unequal our world is.

1 The shaded areas in the pie graphs below show the following:

a the 77% of people around the world who live on less than $10 a day;

b the 24% of people who have no electricity;

c the 8% of people who never get enough to eat, ever – who are starving;

d the 1 in 5 people aged over 15 who can't read or write.

Match the numbers against the pies to the letters above.

1

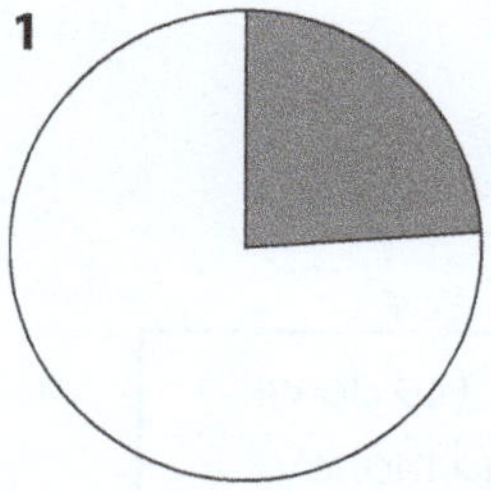

1 = b

2

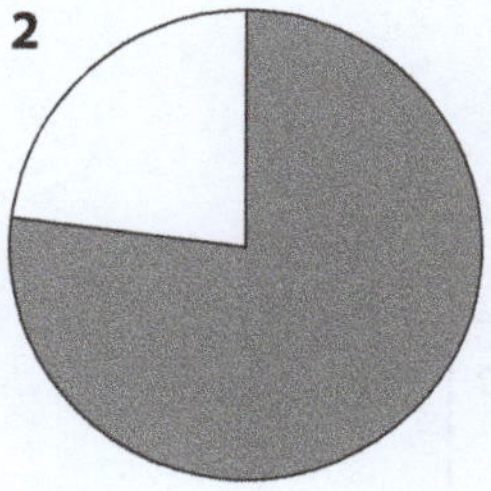

2 = a

3

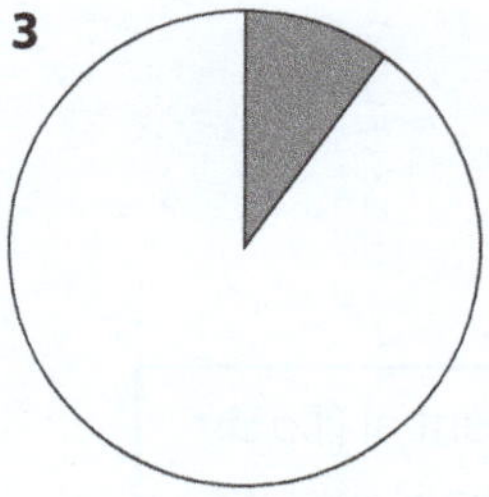

3 = c

4

4

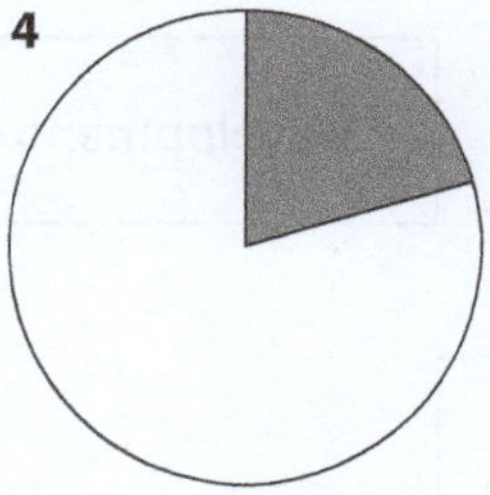

4 = d

2 Decide if each of the following situations describes life in poverty, then tick the correct box.

	poverty	**not poverty**
a living in a home that doesn't have clean safe water	✓	
b having resources worth around $1.90 a day to live on	✓	
c sharing a toilet with another person from your household		✓
d having savings for potential emergencies		✓
e living in a home that has electricity		✓

4.2 So... what is development?

This is about different aspects of development.

1 Complete the spider diagram below, using the words and statements from the box. (You will need to add more 'legs' to the diagram.)

☺ education for everyone	☺ more healthcare for everyone	☺ justice
☺ lower pollution	☺ living longer	☺ more money for the country
☺ equality for women	☺ sustainability	☺ fewer children dying
☺ more jobs		

2 Then add some more ideas of your own.

Answers will vary

Social aspects = education for everyone, more health care for everyone, living longer, and fewer children dying
Political aspects = equality for women and justice
Economic aspects = more jobs, more money for the country
Environmental aspects = lower pollution and sustainability

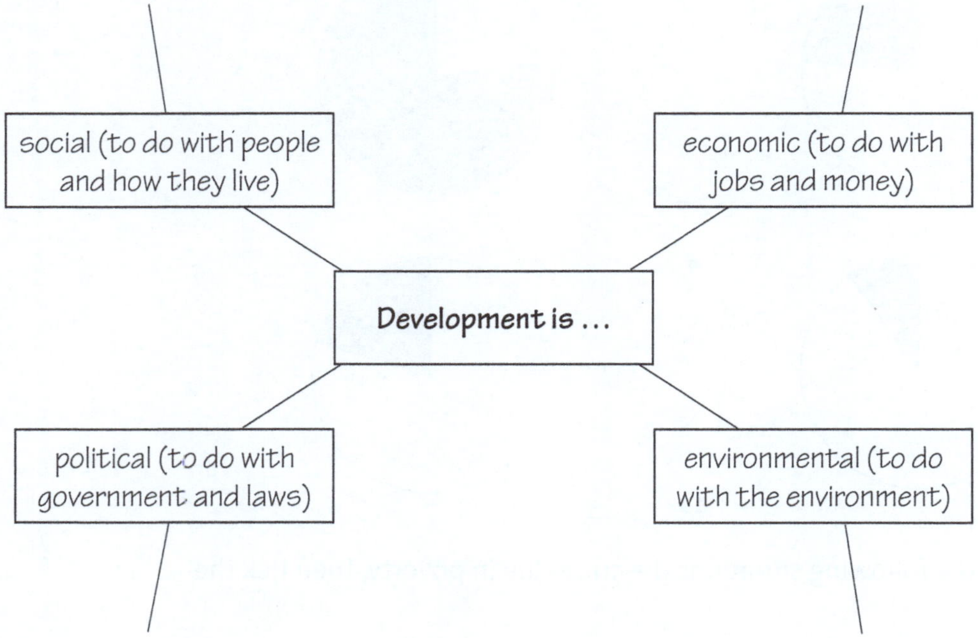

4.3 How is development measured?

This is about identifying developed and developing countries around the world.

1 Finish off these sentences. Use the phrase 'standard of living' in your sentences.

Richer countries are called developed. That means … that a country has a high standard of living.

Poorer ones are called developing. That means … that a country has a low standard of living.

These are shorthand definitions, although the chapter makes it clear that GDP per person does not tell the whole story.

2 If you landed in a strange country and didn't know where you were, how could you tell if it was developed? Think of at least five ways.

This question enables students to dig deeper and to look at development indicators. Possible answers include: looking at the adult literacy rate, the life expectancy, the percentage of the population with access to clean safe water, the number of doctors per 100 000 people, the under-5 mortality rate, the GNI per person, or the percentage of children below age 5 who are underweight.

3 Look at the countries listed below. Some of them are developed, and some are developing.

You need two colours. Use one colour to colour in the developed countries, and the other one to colour in the developing countries. Cross them off the list as you go.

Australia Brazil Canada Egypt Ghana India Japan Kenya New Zealand Peru Somalia Sweden United Kingdom USA Zimbabwe

Developed countries: Australia, Canada, Japan, New Zealand, Sweden, United Kingdom, USA.
Developing countries: Brazil, Egypt, Ghana, India, Kenya, Peru, Somalia, Zimbabwe.

4.4 Malawi: a developing country

Here we look at Sephora's life, and at some of the problems that Malawi faces.

1 Imagine you are Sephora. In your own words, describe what you do during the day.

At 6.15 am I... Students will describe Sephora's day in their own words, drawing on the text on page 73 of **geog.3.**

At 7 am I...

At 1 pm I...

At 6 pm I...

At 7 pm I...

2 Explain what your hopes are for the future. Are they likely to happen? If not, why not?

Students will describe Sephora's hopes for the future in their own words, drawing on the text on page 73 of **geog.3.**

3 Malawi depends more and more on tobacco sales for export earnings. Why might this be a problem in the future?

Although tobacco sales are booming in Africa at the moment, world-wide sales of tobacco are declining. Besides, it is always risky for a nation to rely heavily on one export crop.

4 Do the majority of workers in Malawi earn a living by working in the primary, the secondary, or the tertiary sector? What type of job do they do?

By working in the primary sector. Most of them work in farming.

5 Use the following numbers to complete the text: 4, 64, 18, 51.

Around 51 % of the people in Malawi live in poverty. The median age of the population is 18 and the life expectancy is 64. They have an average of 4 doctors per 100 000 people.

4.5 How did the development gap grow? – part 1

This is about the reasons for the development gap.

1 The paragraphs below are all about why some countries are poorer than others. The words in brackets are all jumbled up though! You need to unscramble them and write them on the lines.

Historical reasons

Many poorer countries were once (cilnoodes) colonised by European countries. The Europeans took raw (atameirls) materials and turned them into finished (gsdoo) goods. They sold these goods back to the poorer country! When the colonisers left, the countries had little (iustrnyd) industry, people didn't have much (edcaution) education or many (sskIli) skills.

Geographical reasons

Some poorer countries have difficult (matescli) climates so they can't grow (fdoo) food.

Social and political reasons

A country has a better chance of developing if it is (ecuesre) secure, but some poorer countries have (sraw) wars. They also have (ropctur) corrupt leaders who make themselves rich while their people live in (rvoypet) poverty.

2 The reasons above can be divided into three groups. Match the titles of the groups with their meanings by drawing linking lines.

historical reasons	reasons that are about natural resources, rainfall, temperature, soils and landscapes
social and political reasons	reasons that are about what happened in the past, like colonisation
geographical reasons	reasons that are about politics and money

(Lines drawn: historical reasons → reasons that are about what happened in the past, like colonisation; social and political reasons → reasons that are about politics and money; geographical reasons → reasons that are about natural resources, rainfall, temperature, soils and landscapes)

3 In the space above each paragraph in the box, you are going to write its title. Use the group titles from question **2**.

4.6 How did the development gap grow? – part 2

This is about the factors that keep the development gap wide.

Here is a list of the Heavily Indebted Poor Countries (HIPCs) that have qualified for and received financial help.

[Note. To qualify for HIPC status a country has to prove that it cannot pay off its debt even after it has received all normal debt assistance.]

Students will need an atlas to identify the African countries from the list.

Benin	Rwanda
Guinea	São Tomé and Príncipe
Guinea- Bissau	Sierra Leone
Honduras	Senegal
Madagascar	Tanzania
Malawi	Uganda
Mali	Zambia
Mauritania	Afghanistan
Mozambique	Burundi
Nicaragua	Centra African Republic
Bolivia	Comoros
Burkina Faso	Republic of Congo
Cameroon	Côte d'Ivoire
Chad	Guyana
Democratic Republic of the Congo	Haiti
Ethiopia	Liberia
the Gambia	Togo
Ghana	
Niger	

Colour in the HIPC countries in Africa on the map above. Then cross them off the list above.

1 Which countries on the list are **not** in Africa?

Honduras, Nicaragua, Bolivia, Afghanistan, Guyana, and Haiti.

2 Can you list at least three things that make it difficult for poor countries to escape poverty?

Answers will vary. Possible answers are: having a corrupt government, being in conflict, having an economy that relies on a few exports, or having a lack of industry.

4.7 Globalisation, development and TNCs

This is about TNCs and their relationship with developing countries.

1 Complete the sentences below. Use the words in the box to help you.

profit	goods	cheaper	Chinese	headquarters	lower	(TNCS)	international

Transnational Corporations TNCs are large companies with international branches. Most have their headquarters in high income countries, but their manufacturing is usually done in developing countries. This is because wages are lower and raw materials are cheaper there, so it costs less to produce goods, and they can make more profit. The world's richest TNCs are American and Chinese.

2 TNCs are responsible for over half of all world trade, and they can have a huge impact on development. But, what does development mean?

Complete the definition:

Development is… a process of change that improves people's lives.

3 To find out how a country is changing, we can study its **development indicators** over time.

a Life expectancy is a useful indicator. Write a definition and then explain how TNCs can have an impact.

Development indicator: Life expectancy

Definition: How many years a newborn baby can expect to live for, on average.

TNCs can impact life expectancy because… workers earn more money which they can use to improve the diet and health of their whole family. The increased income the government earns from taxes can be invested into hospitals, which means more people can be saved from curable diseases.

b Now choose another development indicator. This could be GNI, literacy rate, number of doctors per person – or something else.

Development indicator: .... Answers will vary.

Definition: ....

TNCs can impact this because… ....

4.8 Covid-19 and vaccine inequality

This is about the Covid-19 vaccine.

1 Why can we say that creating a vaccine against Covid-19 was a global effort? List two reasons.

They were developed in different countries, teams around the world helped each other, different high income countries funded the research, many countries agreed to take part in the vaccine trials...

2 This graph shows the total of Covid-19 vaccines administered per 100 people in high-income countries, low-income countries, and in the UK. (Notice that over 200 hundred vaccine doses got administered per 100 people because some people got second doses and boosters).

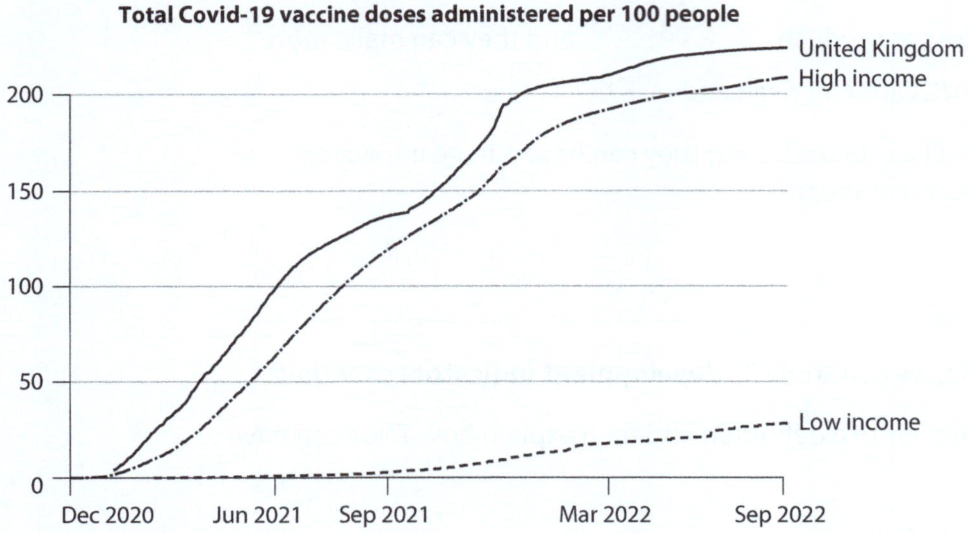

a The graph shows a big difference in the rate at which high-income countries, such as the UK, and low-income countries, vaccinated their populations. Why do you think that is?

High income countries ordered the vaccine in advance, and they ordered more than they needed. Poor countries could not compete with them.

b Looking at the graph, you can see that low-income countries slowly started to get access to more doses of the vaccine. What is the scheme that allowed for that to happen?

COVAX

c As you can see in the graph, the UK was one of the first countries to administer Covid-19 vaccines. In fact, to make that happen, the UK ordered about three times what it needed. Can you list a positive and a negative result of that decision?

Answers will vary. Students might point out that while it helped the UK population, it meant poorer countries did not have access to the vaccine, which meant the virus could spread and mutate.

Escaping from poverty

This is about the different kinds of migrants.

1 Some of the people shown could be called refugees, and some migrants. Is it possible to make a distinction between them? What are your views?

The distinction between economic migrant and political refugee is a difficult one to make. Students' answers will vary depending on their views, but they should be able to recognise that a refugee has been forced to flee from obvious danger, while an economic migrant has moved to look for work or a better life.

4.10 Can we put an end to poverty?

Trade or aid? This looks at the arguments.

1 The arguments in favour of aid or trade to help developing countries has been going on for a long time. Read the arguments for and against below, and then give your opinions.

Arguments in favour of trade

- **Trade** makes a developing country more independent of the aid-giving countries. Aid budgets can always be cut.
- **Trade** helps developing countries to maintain their dignity. Aid can be seen as a form of charity.
- **Trade** establishes a strong impression in the international market.
- **Trade** improves the economic performance of a country while aid money can be misused. Aid can lead to corruption.

Arguments in favour of aid

- **Aid** can go directly to where it is needed, while trade can distribute resources inefficiently. The benefit of trade is mostly confined to an elite group of people within the country.
- **Aid** is not always provided in the form of money, and is sometimes provided through expert advisors. On the other hand, trade needs a good infrastructure of the country to prosper. It is very difficult for the developing countries to maintain a good infrastructure.
- **Aid** allows for money in a given country to be allocated well against need.
- Exposing fragile developing economies to free **trade** is very risky.
- **Trade** requires investment first.
- **Trade** does not necessarily mean **fair trade.**

Aid or trade? Students should read the arguments for and against trade and aid in the worksheet and then decide which of the two helps the developing country more. They may decide that a balance between the two is a good idea, with carefully directed aid establishing the conditions for successful trade.

Our restless planet

5.1 What's Earth like inside?

This is about the three layers that make up the Earth.

1 This diagram shows the layers that make up the Earth.

a Write the words from the box in the rectangles to correctly label the diagram.

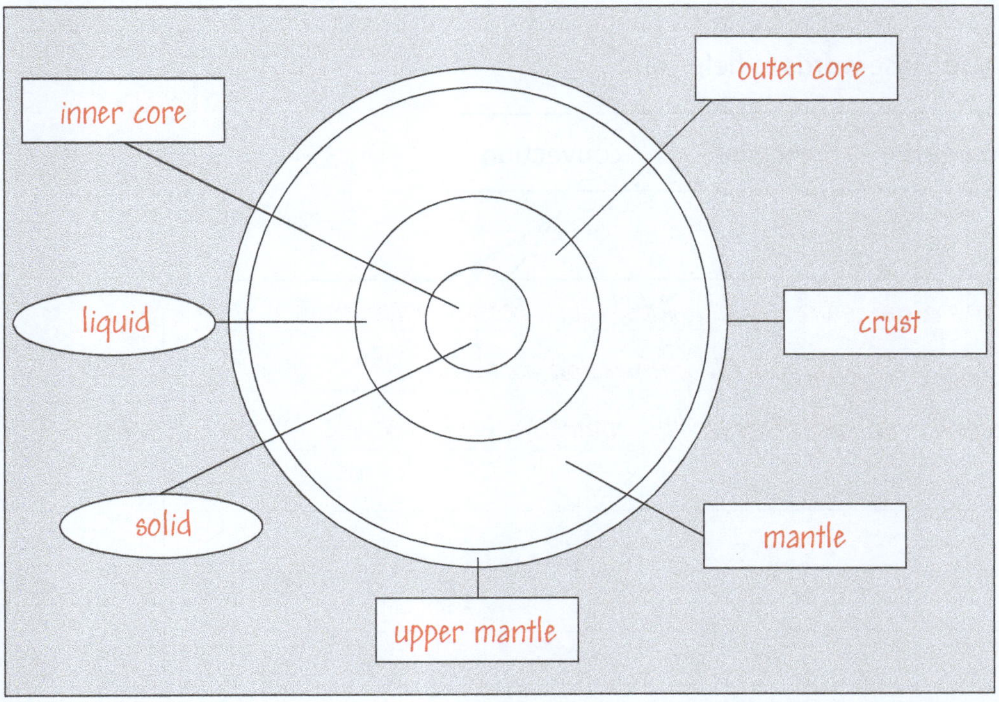

mantle

hard rock

crust

inner core

outer core

b Now colour the inner core yellow, the outer core orange, the mantle brown, and the crust black. Then, add the words **solid** and **liquid** to the diagram.

Now try these...

2 What is the lithosphere composed of? The lithosphere is composed of the crust and upper mantle.

3 a What is the radius of the Earth? The radius of the Earth is 6,371 km

b How can you use this figure to work out the circumference of the Earth? (Clue: think **pi**)

The formula to use to calculate the circumference from the radius is $2\pi r$*, where pi is 3.14159.*

c What is the circumference of the Earth? 40,075 km at the equator and slightly less at the poles.

4 There is continental and oceanic crust. What are the differences between them?

The continental crust (up to 70 km thick) is mainly made of granite and is thicker than the oceanic crust (about 7 km thick) which is mainly made of basalt.

5.2 A cracked Earth?

This is about where the Earth's plates are – and their link with earthquakes and volcanoes.

1 Write a reply to this question. Use these words to help you.

plates	crust	margins	moving	convection

A sample answer could be:

Well, it's because … the Earth's **crust** is broken into slabs, called **plates**, which are **moving** because they are dragged along by powerful **convection** currents in the soft rock below. Where plates push into each other on their **margins**, earthquakes and volcanoes occur.

2 Why don't earthquakes and volcanoes happen in some places?

This could be because they are far from plate margins, whether pushing into each other or moving apart.

3 Why are the Himalayas increasing in height?

This is because the Indo-Australian and Eurasian plates are pushing into each other, so the Himalayas are increasing in height.

4 Why are volcanoes frequent in Iceland?

This is because Iceland lies on the margin of the North American and Eurasian plates.

5 Why are there no major earthquakes in Britain?

There are no major earthquakes in Britain because it lies far from any plate margins.

A closer look at plate movements

This is about how the Earth's plates are moving – and how their movements produce earthquakes, volcanoes, and even mountains!

1 These pictures show the different kinds of plate margins.

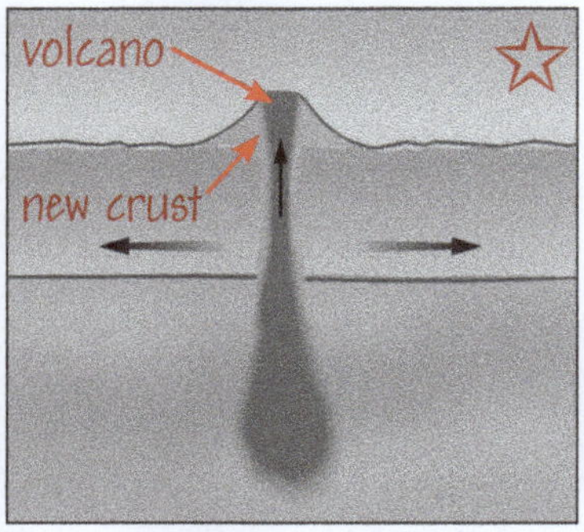

plates are moving apart

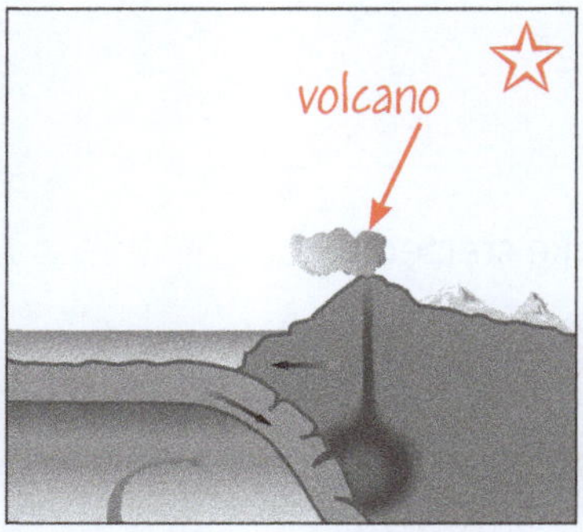

one oceanic plate is going under a continental one

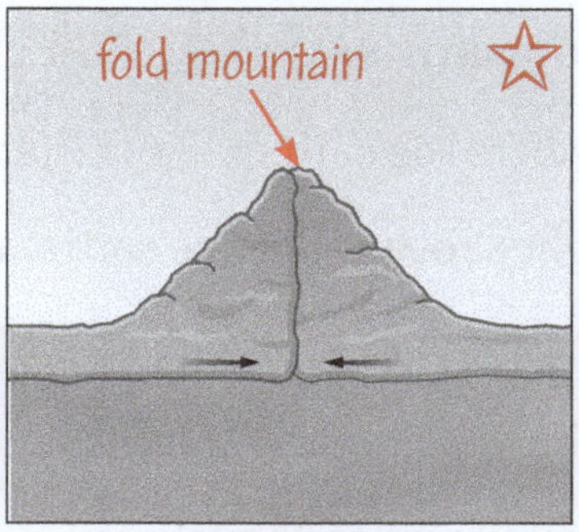

two continental plates pushing into each other

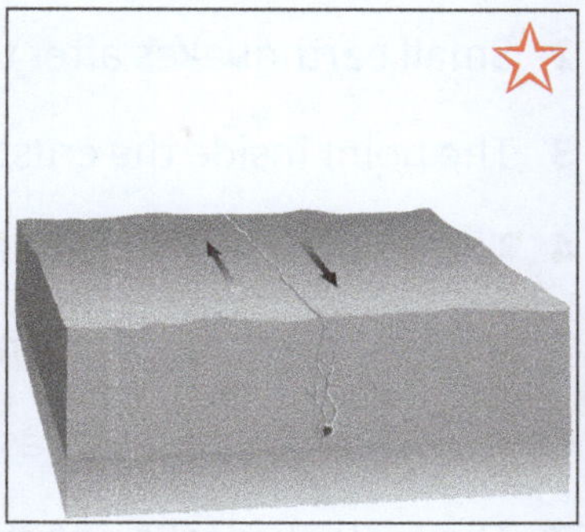

plates are sliding past each other

a Label each diagram. Choose from:

- plates are moving apart
- plates are sliding past each other
- one oceanic plate is going under a continental one
- two continental plates pushing into each other

b Draw a red star on the diagrams where you would expect earthquakes to happen.

c Label any volcanoes you would expect.

d Label the fold mountains.

e Label the new crust that's being formed.

2 Which diagram do you think shows a **constructive** (building) margin? Why?

The diagram on the left shows a constructive margin.

3 Which diagram do you think shows a **destructive** (destroying) margin? Why?

The two middle diagrams show destructive plate margins.

5.4 What is an earthquake?

This is about what earthquakes are, how they are measured, and what damage they do.

Find the correct term to go with each definition.

1 Waves that are made by earthquakes: seismic

2 Small earthquakes after the main one: aftershocks

3 The point inside the crust where the earthquake started: focus

4 The point on the surface right above where the earthquake started: epicentre

5 Amount of energy that an earthquake gives out: magnitude

6 A machine that measures the magnitude of the earthquake: seismometer

7 The scale that tells us how strong an earthquake is: richter

8 A tidal wave caused by earthquakes: tsunami

9 What an earthquake makes the ground do: shake

10 If gas pipes fracture there might be: fires

11 Now find these words in the wordsearch! They could be written horizontally, vertically or diagonally; and forwards or backwards.

	1	2	3	4	5	6	7	8	9	10	11	12	13	14	15
1	r	v	e	e	e	o	u	t	z	w	h	p	u	w	c
2	w	e	f	m	f	a	c	s	u	s	a	x	f	g	j
3	w	p	t	o	v	x	p	u	m	y	e	m	j	w	a
4	v	v	c	e	h	s	c	n	i	d	g	r	q	p	e
5	r	u	z	b	m	f	f	a	m	s	d	e	i	d	x
6	s	i	b	a	b	o	r	m	k	m	r	r	u	f	h
7	q	v	c	t	c	g	m	i	y	p	y	t	d	n	b
8	v	h	u	h	f	x	f	s	w	u	i	n	b	e	m
9	o	d	a	y	t	d	q	c	i	n	o	e	s	e	n
10	e	k	a	h	s	e	v	s	g	e	b	c	k	t	m
11	h	a	e	t	y	o	r	a	q	p	s	i	m	l	r
12	t	p	s	e	i	s	m	i	c	p	w	p	k	f	e
13	s	k	c	o	h	s	r	e	t	f	a	e	c	x	e
14	d	x	y	f	x	c	x	v	n	d	p	s	n	k	u
15	b	u	z	p	p	v	h	o	h	c	l	j	y	y	r

The words and positions for the wordsearch are as follows:

1 seismic, 12 down, 3 across E
2 aftershocks, 13 down, 11 across W
3 focus, 2 down, 5 across SW
4 epicentre, 13 down, 12 across N
5 magnitude, 12 down, 7 across NE
6 seismometer, 11 down, 11 across NW
7 richter, 5 down, 1 across SE
8 tsunami, 1 down, 8 across S
9 shake, 10 down, 5 across W
10 fires, 6 down, 14 across NW

5.5 An earthquake in Southwest China

This is about the damage caused in the Sichuan earthquake of 2008.

The earthquake factfile	
date	Monday 12 May 2008
time	2.28 pm
magnitude	7.9 on the Richter scale
epicentre	in mountains in Sichuan Province, Southwest China
damage	over 87 000 dead over 370 000 injured, and at least 5 million left homeless in Sichuan Province
financial cost	nearly £120 billion

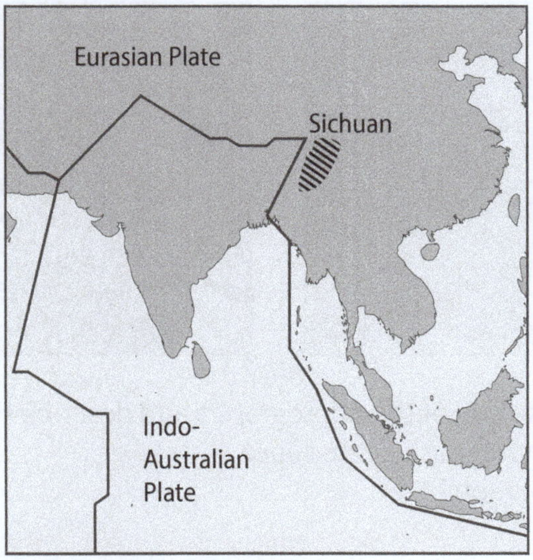

1 Using the information from the map and the factfile, add words to the speech bubble to complete what the two people are saying.

The two answers will be based on the text in unit 5.5. Examples could be:

This is what caused the earthquake:
rock slipped downwards at a fault where two plates meet.

The damage was terrible.
Nearly half a million dead or injured, five million left homeless, and many millions of farm animals killed.

2 Look at the table below. Put a tick in the column to show if what happened could have been stopped or not.

Event	Could not be stopped	Could be stopped
1 The two plates were colliding and causing a lot of strain	✓	
2 On 12 May the strain got too much	✓	
3 At 2.28 in the afternoon the ground shook	✓	
4 Buildings in Beichuan Middle School collapsed		✓
5 Rock slipped as much as 12 metres along the fault	✓	
6 Parents blamed local officials for erecting poorly built schools		✓
7 Students and teachers were crushed to death		✓
8 Over 87 000 people died		✓

5.6 Tsunami!

This is about the damage tsunamis do to the environment, the economy, and people.

A

B

C

D

1 Choose one of the photographs and describe the damage that you can see. Write the letter of the photograph in the space.
Photograph [ ]

Answers will vary depending on which photo the student selects.

2 Complete the table below to describe the damage caused to the environment, the economy and people.

Photograph A
Natural = trees and farmland
Economic = boats and shops
Social = homes and possessions

Photograph B

Photograph C

Photograph D

5.7 Volcanoes

This is about what volcanoes are, and the damage an eruption can do.

Volcanoes happen on the edges of plates, where one plate goes under another. Sometimes the plate suddenly starts moving and you get a new volcano where there wasn't one before.

Students can draw on text and artwork in Unit 5.7 for inspiration.

This is what happened in Mexico …

Draw a picture for each of the boxes in this cartoon strip.

1 It was 1943. In a flat maize (corn on the cob) field in Mexico…

2 … smoke and ash were seen coming from the ground.

3 The ground cracked and there was a terrible smell like rotten eggs.

4 By the next morning the cone of ash was as tall as a house.

5 Over the next year the cone built up with layers of ash and lava to make a new volcano. It was named after the nearest village – Paricutin.

6 The mountain erupted for 9 years! By the end it had covered 10 square miles in lava and caused over 1000 people to die.

7 The lava and ash caused damage during the eruption but left the soil fertile (good and rich) so now lots of crops can be grown and livestock (farm animals) graze the land.

8 Now Paricutin is nearly 400 metres high.

5.8 The most dangerous volcano in the world?

This is about a potential eruption of Mount Vesuvius.

1 This map shows one plate sinking under a different one, which gives rise to Italy's volcanoes. What are each of the two plates called?

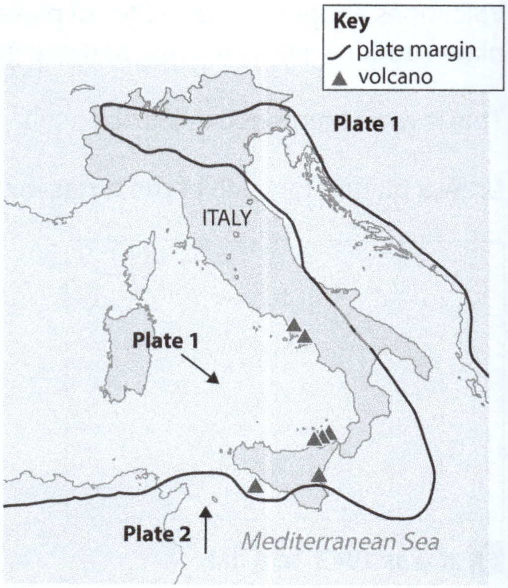

Plate 1: Eurasian Plate

Plate 2: African Plate

2 Imagine that you are living close to Mount Vesuvius when scientists give warning of an eruption. You are asked to evacuate the area in less than three days. Complete the sentences: Answers will vary.

I have to… Students could mention that in case of evacuation they'd have to go somewhere else in Italy.

My main concern is… Students could say they'd be concerned about the plans of evacuation.

When the volcanic eruption is over, I… Students could say that when the eruption is over, they might not be able to go back home.

3 Look at this photo of Mount Vesuvius, taken from Naples.
How different do you think it would look after a volcanic eruption?
What would have changed?

Answers will vary, but students should be able to identify that, if pyroclastic flows slid down the slopes, they would destroy everything in their way, and the areas affected by the eruption would be buried under ash and pumice.

5.9 So why live in a danger zone?

Here we consider issues around living in an earthquake zone.

1 Since 1836 there have been 5 major earthquakes in the San Francisco area, plus 15 smaller but damaging earthquakes. The probability of a magnitude 7 earthquake in the next 30 years is about 75 per cent. You have been offered an exciting long-term job in San Francisco. Give the arguments for and against accepting the job.

For The arguments for going will include the fact that modern building techniques mean that the amount of damage could be small, and the expected earthquake might not be severe.

Against The arguments against are that the odds are in favour of an earthquake in the relatively short term, and it could be severe involving loss of life.

What would **you** decide? Why? Students' final decisions will vary.

2 Geothermal energy is renewable and continuous. Ninety per cent of Iceland's energy is produced this way. Why is it more difficult to produce geothermal energy in the UK?

Access to 'hot rocks' is much easier in Iceland than in the UK, where drilling would have to be deeper and would cost more.

3 In 2022 there was an earthquake in Japan, and the following year there was an earthquake in Türkiye-Syria. Earthquakes occur often in Japan, while they are a lot less common in Türkiye and Syria. Also, Türkiye and Syria are poorer countries than Japan.

The Japan earthquake recorded 7.4 on the Richter scale and there was a loss of life of 3 people. The Türkiye and Syria earthquake recorded 7.8 on the Richter scale and there was a loss of life of over 55,000.

Can you account for the difference in the death toll between the two earthquakes when they were of a similar magnitude?

Japan is more prepared for earthquakes than Türkiye and Syria, so many buildings are designed to resist earthquakes. And Japan is an affluent country.

Türkiye and Syria were unprepared for an earthquake, and Syria is one of the poorest countries in the world.

About Russia

6.1 Meet Russia!

Tip!
Use your imagination, as wel as facts about the country!

Here you will explain a little more about Russia.

1 The overview shown on page 109 in **geog.3** gives six facts about Russia. Imagine that you are a visitor to Russia. Write a postcard home explaining what you expect your visit to Russia to be like.

A postcard from Russia

Answers will vary depending upon which facts the pupils choose to write about. Expect pupils to explain and contextualise what they expect to see (e.g. I can't believe how empty much of Russia is. We have travelled for miles and not seen anybody. There are also areas that you cannot reach by road or rail – scary!)

6.2 What are Russia's main physical features?

Here you will find out more about Russia's 'Mother Volga'.

The Volga River is Europe's longest river, over 2200 miles long, and is seen as the 'national river of Russia'. The river starts north-west of Moscow and flows out in to the Caspian Sea. Eleven out of the twenty largest cities of Russia, including its capital Moscow, are situated in the Volga basin. Over 40% of Russia's population live near it. It is used for transport, hydro-electric power production, and irrigation. Some of the world's largest reservoirs can be found along its banks. It is a major source of Russia's water. The river plays a major part in the day to day life of the Russian people and is known as 'Mother Volga'.

Large quantities of wheat are grown in the fertile river valley, and an important petroleum industry is based in the Volga valley. Other minerals that are found include natural gas, salt, and potash, which is used as a fertiliser. The river's delta and the nearby Caspian Sea offer rich fishing grounds. The Volga also has a number of holiday destinations along its route, and many cruises take place along its course. Nearly the entire length of the River Volga is navigable from about March until mid-December.

1 'Without the River Volga, Russia would not have become such a powerful country'. To what extent do you agree with this statement? Give reasons for your answer.

Students should identify the River Volga's contribution to Russia's economy, which in turn gives the country its powerful status. A variety of answers are possible, such as the river provides transport which means that the country can import and export goods; the river helps provide HEP without which its industries would not have developed; the cruises bring many tourists who spend money and therefore help the Russian economy to grow. Students should also state whether or not they agree with the statement.

2 What threats do you think the River Volga could be faced with? Give reasons for your answer.

Students are likely to focus on the threats to the quality of water in the river. Students may identify threats from the cruise boats or fertiliser seepage from fields, for example. Other possible answers may revolve around water extraction for urban, industrial and agricultural use, or threats to fish species due to possible over-fishing.

6.3 Russia's climate zones and biomes

Here you will find out more about Russia's varied climate and vegetation.

1 What is permafrost? What problems may this cause for people?

Permafrost is a layer of soil below ground which is always frozen, even in summer.
Problems are likely to relate to difficulties in farming, the construction of buildings or roads, or the laying of electricity or water pipes.

2 Fill in the gaps in this table. Use the information on pages 112–113 in **geog.3** to help you.

Biome	Main features	Animals
Tundra	Covered in ice and snow in winter In summer the surface of the soil thaws	Musk ox, Arctic foxes, polar bears, brown bears, reindeer, ermine
Taiga	Coniferous forest Trees with needles not leaves	Bears, wolves, Siberian tigers
Temperate forest	Mixture of deciduous and coniferous trees	Wolves, foxes, deer and squirrels
Steppe	Grassland Fertile soil Used for agriculture	Cattle, hamsters, mice
Mountain	Colder Thinner soils No trees above the tree line	Mountain goats, deer, lynx and foxes

3 Which of the biomes would you like to visit? Give reasons for your answer.

Answers will vary but reasons should relate to the details identified in question 2.

6.4 What about the Russian people?

Here you will find out more about Russia's 146 million people.

1 Why is the population denser in the European part of Russia?

The population is denser in the European part of Russia because the climate is milder and therefore it is more pleasant to live there, and easier to farm the land.

2 Why are large areas of Siberia empty of people?

Siberia is so very cold and also very remote with few roads. It is difficult to travel and farm there which means that not many people can live there.

3 Study pages 114 and 115 in **geog.3**. Link the numbers below to a fact about Russia's people. Write the facts in the space next to the number. The first one has been done to help you.

Number	Fact
14%	Percentage of Russia's population who have just enough to survive
75%	*Percentage of Russia's population who live in urban areas*
5.5 million	*St Petersburg's population*
78%	*Percentage of Russia's population who live in European Russia*
185	*Number of ethnic groups in Russia*
146 million	*Russia's population estimate*
81%	*Percentage of the population who call themselves Russian*

6.5 A tour of European Russia

Here you will explore Sochi, a tourist resort on the shores of the Black Sea.

Sochi is the biggest resort town on what's known as the 'Russian Riviera'

Unlike most of Russia, Sochi has a subtropical climate. Its summers are warm or hot, and its winters are mild

You can enjoy beautiful sunsets over the sea, and admire the snow-capped mountains

There are plenty of smart restaurants and outdoor cafes – Sochi has everything you could wish for in a resort

Sochi has the backdrop of the Caucasus Mountains, both pebble and sandy beaches, and the ski resort is 30 miles away

Sochi has more than 200 days of sunshine a year, with an average temperature of above 14 degrees Celsius

Sochi, transformed by the 2014 Winter Olympic Games it hosted, has turned into a year-round resort

Greater Sochi is an incredibly long city – 145 km along the Black Sea Coast

More than three million people visited Sochi during 2014 – the year it hosted the Olympic Games

Sochi: palm-fringed seaside resorts, spectacular ski facilities and a superb conference venue

1 Using the map and an atlas describe the location of Sochi. Remember to use geographical terms in your answer.

Sochi is found in south-western Russia. It is on the eastern shores of the Black Sea and west of the Caucasus Mountains. It lies generally south of Moscow.

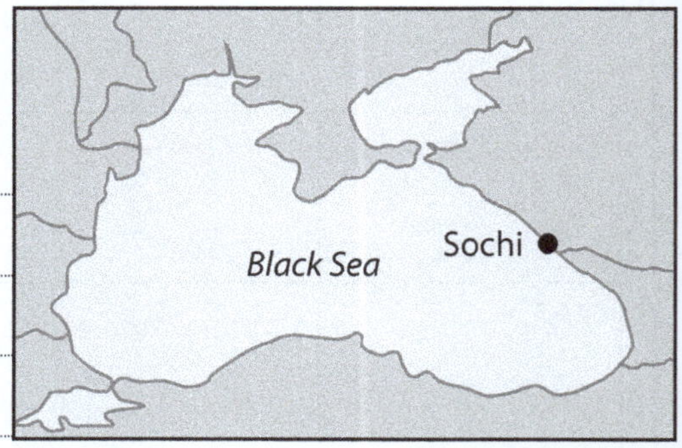

2 The Russian Prime Minister is expected to chair a conference on the development of tourist facilities and mountain skiing infrastructure in the Sochi area. You have been asked to prepare a 100 word news bulletin to help promote the resort. Use the information above to help you write your bulletin.

Tip! Remember to be persuasive!

The answer should be exactly one hundred words and should use facts given to promote the area for both beach and mountain tourists.

Climate change in Yakutia

This is about the features and climate of the Siberian region of Yakutia in Russia.

1 Using an atlas, add the following features to the map:

a the Yakutia district (colour it orange)

b the river Lena (use blue)

c the Arctic Circle (draw a dotted line)

d the city of Yakutsk.

Tip!
Make sure you label all the features you add to the map.

The map should look like this once the students are done:

2 Study this climate graph for Yakutsk. A few things are missing!

Using the data from the table, try to complete it by:

a adding the months of the year to the X axis

b adding suitable numbers to each Y axis (average temperature on the left, and precipitation on the right.)

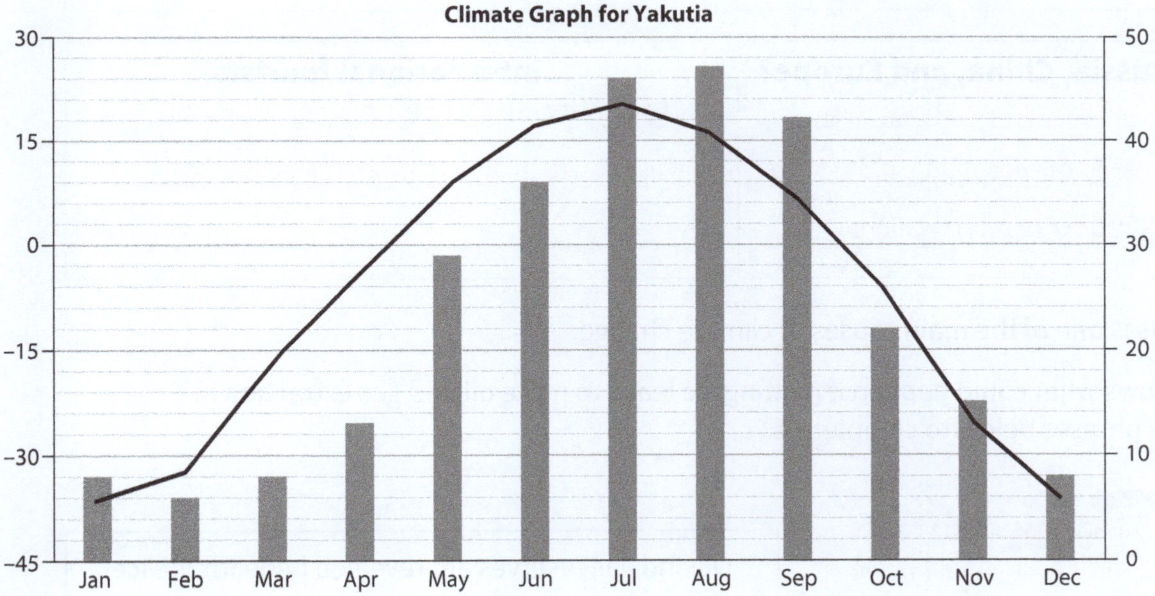

See graph. Students should have added data the Y axes as shown below. Accurate placement of the data at equidistant points is important, on both sides.

	Jan.	Feb.	Mar.	Apr.	May	June	July	Aug.	Sep.	Oct.	Nov.	Dec.
Avg. Temp °C	−36.3	−32.2	−17.1	−3.6	8	17	20	16	6.4	−6.8	−25.1	−35.9
Precipitation mm	8	6	8	13	29	36	46	47	42	22	15	8

What is Russia doing in the Arctic Ocean?

This is about the impacts of melting ice in the Arctic.

1 Scientists have noticed that more ocean ice is melting in Arctic summers, and this has been linked to climate change.

How will melting ice affect...

...polar bears?
They rely on ocean ice to reach their main food, seals. Melting ice is forcing them to scavenge on land.

...ocean ecosystems?
Food chains will be harmed by oil spills and by the destructive process of extracting oil and gas.

...the Arctic fishing industry?
There will be more access to fish in the ice-free parts of the ocean, particularly in summer.

...Russian oil companies?
They will have more access to oil and gas from reserves which were once under the ice. If it is extracted and sold, their profits could increase.

...traders in Russia, China, and Europe?
Goods could be transported on an ice-free ocean between Russia, Europe, and China. More opportunities for trading between nations.

...international tourists?
They will be able to visit the north pole on ships in summer when there is no sea ice.

2 Burning fossil fuels is one of the main causes of climate change.

This flow chart shows what could happen if melting ice leads to more oil and gas extraction in the Arctic. Use the phrases below to complete it.

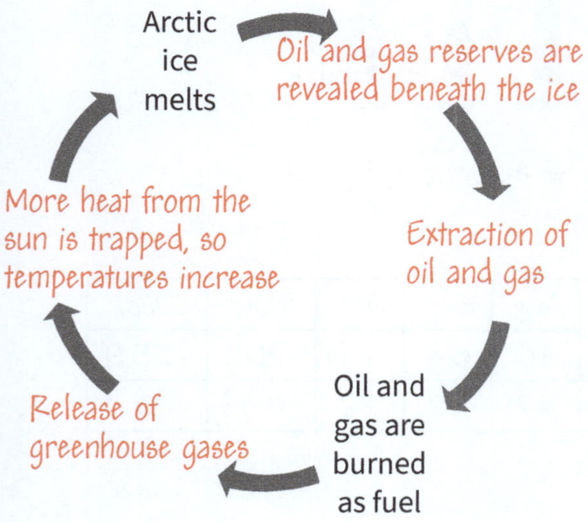

- Oil and gas reserves are revealed beneath the ice
- Release of greenhouse gases
- Extraction of oil and gas
- More heat from the sun is trapped, so temperatures increase

The Middle East

7.1 Introducing the Middle East

It's time to find out some facts about the Middle East.

1 Use the map on page 124 in **geog.3** to answer the following

a If you travelled in a straight line from Cyprus to the border between Yemen and Oman, which countries would you pass through?

Cyprus, Lebanon, Syria, Jordan and Saudi Arabia.

b Which two countries are found due south of Iraq?

Saudi Arabia and Yemen.

c Which two countries lie south-east of Qatar?

United Arab Emirates (UAE) and Oman.

2 Write 'True' or 'False' in the box after each of these sentences.

a The Middle East is where Asia, Europe and Africa meet. *True*

b The United Arab Emirates is made up of eight small states. *False*

c Yemen is an island nation. *False*

d The Middle East's large oil reserves are mainly in Egypt. *False*

e Islam is the dominant religion of the Middle East. *True*

3 A region is an area that shares a feature – such as a distinct climate, or a language, or a mountain range. What do you think defines the Middle East as a region?

The Middle East has a shared history as most of it used to belong to, or be controlled by, the Islamic Ottoman Empire.

4 Research one country in the Middle East. Find out five fun facts and see if a partner can guess which country you have researched. *Answers will vary.*

Fact 1 ....

Fact 2 ....

Fact 3 ....

Fact 4 ....

Fact 5 ....

7.2 The Middle East: physical geography

Here you will find out more about the Red Sea.

1 Read these facts about the Red Sea. Design a fact-filled poster that tells people what the Red Sea is like. You must include a map, and be as creative as you can!

The region surrounding the Red Sea is one of the hottest, driest areas on the planet.

The Red Sea is an extension of the Indian Ocean, located between Africa and Asia.

It is around 190 miles across at its widest point, and about 1,200 miles long.

Intense heat and little precipitation means the water in the Red Sea evaporates quickly.

The Red Sea is home to over two hundred types of coral reefs.

Water in the Red Sea has very clear visibility and warm temperatures throughout the year.

It attracts divers, photographers, marine scientists, and tourists from all over the world.

Cargo vessels, oil tankers, fishing boats, and cruise liners are all found sailing its waters.

Desalination plants along its shores mean that its water can be purified for drinking.

Sea water is also used for industry, such as cement works and oil refineries.

10% of fish species in the Red Sea are not found anywhere else on earth.

Minerals build up in the Red Sea water as it evaporates so the sea is very saline, or salty.

To the north, the Red Sea splits in two, the Gulf of Suez and the Gulf of Aqaba.

The Suez Canal connects the Mediterranean Sea with the Red Sea's Gulf of Suez

Answers will vary but should portray some of the features described above. A map must be included on the poster.

7.3 The Middle East: climate zones and biomes

Here you will find out more about the Middle East's climate and vegetation.

1 The statements below explain why the Middle East does not get much rain. But they are in the wrong order! Write the missing numbers in the table to show the correct order. Use page 128 in **geog.3** to help you.

Order	Climate fact
1	The land at the Equator gets hot.
8	It descends again at the Tropics, around 30° north and south of the Equator.
2	The land heats the air.
4	The air cools, and its water vapour condenses.
5	Heavy rain falls at the Equator.
3	The warm air rises around the Equator.
7	The risen air, which has lost all its moisture, gets pushed out of the way.
9	The air is dry in the Middle East region.
6	As the warm air rises, colder air moves in to take its place.
10	Dry air means little or no rain.

2 Circle the correct biome for the following sentences.

a Bears and hyena are found here — Desert — (Mediterranean areas) — Semi-arid areas

b Plants may have spiky leaves — (Desert) — Mediterranean areas — Semi-arid areas

c Scorpions are found here — (Desert) — Mediterranean areas — Semi-arid areas

d Sometimes called Steppe — Desert — Mediterranean areas — (Semi-arid areas)

e A few trees may be found here — Desert — Mediterranean areas — (Semi-arid areas)

f Cypresses are found here — Desert — (Mediterranean areas) — Semi-arid areas

3 Write fifteen words to explain how climate affects natural vegetation.

Answers will vary, but should be exactly fifteen words long. One example is:

Trees need quite a lot of rainfall. The lack of rainfall makes their growth difficult.

7.4 The people, and economies

Here you will find out more about the Middle East's population.

1 Write down the correct answer to these questions.

a What is the combined population of Iraq and Iran to the nearest million? 130 million

b Which country has a population almost exactly six times bigger than Qatar? Syria

c Which country has a population eleven times bigger than London? Egypt

2 What is the biggest ethnic group in the Middle East? List five countries where this ethnic group makes up the majority of the population.

Arabs are the biggest ethnic group in the Middle East. Egypt, Jordan, Lebanon, Syria, Iran, Kuwait, Saudi Arabia, Bahrain, Qatar, the UAE, Oman, and Yemen are all mainly Arab.

3 Who am I? Identify the two Middle Eastern countries from the facts given below.

I have five letters
I am in the south
I border the Red Sea
I have a population of 30.3 million
Answer Yemen

I am east of the Mediterranean Sea
Kurds live in the north
My capital is Tehran
Most people speak Persian
Answer Iran

4 Middle East Challenge!

Solve the word square below.

arabs
christian
egypt
iraq
islam
jews
kurdistan
kuwait
lebanon
mecca
muslim
oman
qatar
riyadh
turkey

h	n	n	t	e	x	i	z	o	o	c	r	r	a	p
z	a	p	a	p	u	t	l	z	y	z	z	x	t	y
y	i	m	v	t	y	n	d	h	g	w	j	e	g	a
u	t	l	v	m	s	g	f	c	u	i	u	n	j	c
r	s	e	u	r	k	i	e	y	b	q	o	o	g	v
j	i	l	a	o	b	i	d	u	j	n	t	m	c	n
e	r	y	r	l	c	b	b	r	a	m	a	l	s	i
w	h	j	a	u	i	x	e	b	u	k	j	o	z	t
s	c	z	t	d	i	r	e	k	u	k	m	y	i	u
r	c	t	a	r	h	l	a	w	y	a	t	s	o	r
c	g	k	q	j	p	f	a	q	n	g	b	r	k	k
m	e	c	c	a	s	i	f	r	x	a	g	z	l	e
l	c	a	s	w	t	n	z	m	r	v	c	k	h	y
o	m	m	l	c	k	l	n	a	f	w	q	l	h	n
j	g	u	m	u	s	l	i	m	l	v	s	k	a	a

(Over, Down, Direction)

Word	(Over, Down, Direction)
ARABS	(9, 14, NE)
CHRISTIAN	(2, 9, N)
EGYPT	(8, 5, NW)
IRAQ	(6, 8, SE)
ISLAM	(15, 7, W)
JEWS	(1, 6, S)
KURDISTAN	(11, 9, NW)
KUWAIT	(11, 8, SW)
LEBANON	(7, 10, NE)
MECCA	(1, 12, E)
MUSLIM	(4, 15, E)
OMAN	(13, 8, SW)
QATAR	(4, 11, N)
RIYADH	(1, 5, SE)
TURKEY	(15, 8, S)

Challenges in the Arabian Peninsula

Here you will find out more about the world's biggest peninsula!

1 Label the map below with three facts about the Arabian Peninsula.

Answers to Question 1 will vary.

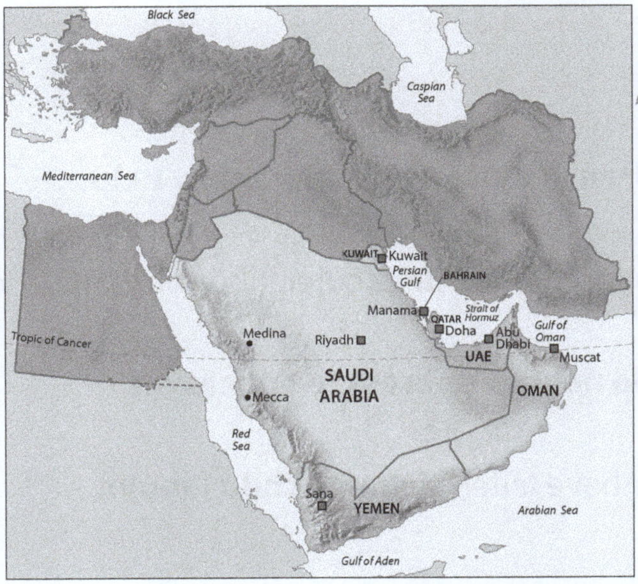

Fact 1

Fact 2

Fact 3

2 The Arabian Peninsula faces a storm of challenges. Look at the challenges listed below, and write at least two ways of tackling each of them. Answers will vary. Here are some examples:

Water stress: desalination of sea water, cleaning of waste water so that it can be used for crops, cloud seeding, increase in water charges to prevent waste.

Food risk: giving grants to companies to turn desert into farmland, investing in farmland abroad to import food, using hydroponics.

A fall in demand for oil and gas: using money from oil and gas sales to buy shares in other countries, using money from oil and gas sales to diversify their own economies, developing high-tech companies, and encouraging people to start their own businesses.

7.6 Conflict in the Middle East

Here you will find out some more about the conflicts found in the Middle East.

1 Conflict always leads to people becoming refugees. What do you think a refugee is?

A refugee (in the context of political conflict) is a person who has fled their own country because they have been persecuted and felt threatened because of their race, religion, nationality or politics, or because they are trying to escape war.

Over 8.6 million children in **Syria** need **emergency help**.

2.6 million of these children **have fled** to neighbouring countries **in search of safety**.

Over a third of them **do not have access to education.**

An **increasing number** have fallen victim to **child labour.**

2 Read the information above.

Look at some support options given in the table below and rank them 1–5 with number 1 being, in your view, the most urgent. Answers will vary.

RANK	Type of Support
	Provide nutritious food for Syrian children
	Offer permanent resettlement to families in other countries
	Provide doctors
	Support education in Syrian refugee camps
	Provide clean water to refugee camps

3 Explain in detail why you have chosen your number 1. Why do you think it will best support Syrian children through this crisis?

Students should offer clear explanations as to why they have ranked their number one choice for support for Syrian children. For example: *I have chosen doctors as the number one priority. Without doctors, children will become ill and may not survive. If they do not survive, then Syria will not have a large workforce in the future to help the country to develop out of its crisis.*

Your own notes...

5th edition

geog.3 workbook

answer book

This answer book gives you vital support for the geog.3 workbook. Each page matches the workbook and the answers are written in colour, so they're easy and quick to use for marking or reference.

geog.123 is a comprehensive course that matches the National Curriculum at Key Stage 3.

Did you know?

- The summit of Mount Everest is made of limestone …
- … which formed on the ocean floor!

Did you know?

- We throw out over 500 million small electrical items a year, in the UK.

geog.3 workbook
ISBN 978 0 19 848993 1
geog.3 workbook – pack of 10
ISBN 978 0 19 848992 4

Printed on paper produced from sustainable forests.

OXFORD UNIVERSITY PRESS
www.oup.com

How to get in touch:
web www.oxfordsecondary.com
email schools.enquiries.uk@oup.com
tel +44 (0)1536 452620

FSC MIX Paper from responsible sources FSC® C011748

ISBN 978-0-19-848994-8
9 780198 489948